The Magic of Vajrayana

The Magic of Vajrayana

Ken McLeod

Unfettered Mind Media

Pragmatic Buddhism

Windsor, California

To request permissions, contact the publisher at info@unfetteredmind.org

Unfettered Mind Media
www.unfetteredmind.org

Printed in the United States of America

Library of Congress Control Number: 2023910556

ISBN 979-8-98617-110-4 (hardcover)

9 8 7 6 5 4 3 2 1

First edition

Cover photo: Steph Nikora
Book design: VJB/Scribe
Printed by McNaughton & Gunn

to the Dark Lord
who dwells
under the sandalwood tree
with a single trunk
in the Cool Grove
in the south-east

Experience arises like magic.
If you practice like magic
You awaken like magic
Through the power of faith.

—NIGUMA

CONTENTS

ACKNOWLEDGEMENTS AND PERMISSIONS

Numerous people have contributed to this book: Jon Parmenter, Ruth Gilbert, Donna McLaughlin, Sarah Harding, Ingrid McLeod, Stephen Batchelor, James Shaheen, Hokai Sobol, Majda Jurich, Joan Duncan Oliver, Jim Wilson, Claudia Hansson, Ulrich Küstner, Ann Craig, Rob Schmidt, and Stuart Goodnick.

Some of these people helped to clarify practice points. Others pointed out problems or inaccuracies in the text. Still others provided me with friendship and encouragement. More than a few helped me in all three ways.

Janaki Symon's editing skills helped shape the manuscript into its final form. A team of proofreaders, Trudy Gold, Bill Butcher, Jitendra Pant, John Munroe, Larry Akey, and Marti Early, ensured that the manuscript was as clean as possible. Nancy Hawkekotte kindly applied her editing skills to polish the manuscript. Ann Braun Wheatley's keen eye found the right cover. Valerie Caldwell designed the book.

To all these people I am deeply grateful.

My thanks, also, to Walter Mosley, who kindly gave permission for the excerpts from his novel *The Long Fall*, to Steph Nikora for her permission to use her photograph for the cover, and to Sugarcube Studios Ltd. for processing the image.

Ken McLeod

INTRODUCTION

About twenty-five hundred years ago, a young prince in a small kingdom in northern India set out on a spiritual quest — how to live at peace in a life shaped by old age, illness, and death. He gave up everything: his family, his position in society, and every form of conventional success. After much training and hardship he found a way. His understanding and what he passed on to those who sought his counsel gave rise to the collection of religions that we know today as Buddhism.

When I set out to seek answers to my own spiritual questions, it was this pragmatic approach that drew me. More by chance than design, I came to study and practice in the Tibetan tradition, rather than Zen or Theravada. In Tibetan Buddhism I found Vajrayana and entered a world that I did not know existed — a world in which magic was and still is widely practiced, a world in which magic is a path to spiritual understanding.

This book is about the magic of Vajrayana. It is about the practice of that magic. It is also about coming to see, experience, and know life directly — free from mediation by the conceptual mind. In other words, it is about a mystical path, the mystical path of Vajrayana.

Vajrayana is not without its challenges. Its forms, practices, and rituals evolved out of the sorcery cults and religions of ancient India, where it originated, and Tibet, where it has been transmitted from generation to generation for over a thousand years. It is complex, multi-faceted, and deeply entwined with those cultures.

The literature of Vajrayana is itself enormous. Hundreds, if not thousands, of volumes of texts and commentaries were brought from

India to Tibet in two waves — the first in and about the 8th century, the second in the 11th and 12th centuries. Over the last thousand years, Vajrayana in Tibet has given rise to numerous lineages and traditions, each of them with their own vast collections of empowerments, practice texts, commentaries, philosophical treatises, and rituals.

This book is a distillation of my understanding and experience of spiritual practice in the Tibetan Vajrayana tradition. It is not a philosophical or academic book. It favors practice over theory, the spirit of practice over technical details, and methods over results. It includes practices that I have done for many years, what I came to understand through them, and what I learned from teaching them to others.

In coming to this tradition many of us are confronted with a host of questions. What does it mean to see a living person, your teacher, as buddha? What is the relationship between prayer and meditation? How does a deity bring about ecstasy, insight, compassion, wisdom, or other spiritual qualities? Why all the gods? Why all the rituals? And what does a protector do? These are the kinds of questions I address here.

This book is intended for three groups of people: those currently practicing Vajrayana, those interested in practicing Vajrayana, and those whose lives have cracked open. For the first, I offer my experience and understanding in the hope that it will clarify your own practice. For the second, I give you a taste of what practice in this tradition may involve. For the third, whether you experienced some kind of awakening, your life took an unexpected turn, or you are lost beyond words, another's path may unveil something that speaks to yours.

Take a moment now to consider what brought you to spiritual practice. Was it a possibility that you sensed or knew when you were quite young, but lost or forgot as life unfolded? Was it a spontaneous awakening, unexpected and unbidden? Was it an existential shock or personal tragedy that stripped conventional life of all meaning? Was it an intimation of mystery — the miracle of love or compassion, for instance — or an experience or insight beyond the conventional order? Was it a wish to answer the deep questions of life, "Why am I here?" or "What is life?" Was it a need to meet or comprehend your own struggles, or the struggles of others? Perhaps you came through another discipline — medicine, science, sport, art, or craft — and you saw that it pointed to something beyond the discipline itself. Whatever the reason, keep it in mind and hold it in your heart as you read these pages.

In one respect, mystical practice is no different from any other discipline. You need teachers. Whatever your level of interest, whatever your natural ability, a discipline involves learning and training. You need to learn or be shown what is possible. You need to develop skills and build capabilities. And you need to know when you are stuck, what to do about it, and where the dangers lie. As in other disciplines, you may learn these facets of practice from one person or from various people. You may have a long association with one teacher or a crucial seed may be planted in a single meeting with someone you never meet again. You may find a teacher through your own efforts or a teacher may find you. However the connection comes about, a teacher embodies in some way the essence of mystical practice, a knowing that is unmediated by the conceptual mind. That knowing is the vajra in Vajrayana.

The Meaning of Vajrayana

The original vajra was a lightning bolt, a weapon associated with Indra, the Vedic rain and thunder god. According to tradition, a pernicious titan drove Indra from his heavenly abode. Under the protection of powerful magic, the titan could not be defeated by ordinary weapons. Indra and the other gods prevailed on a deeply virtuous sage, asking him to give up his life and allow them to forge a weapon from his bones. He agreed. The virtue of the sage was such that the weapon so fashioned, the vajra, could destroy anything and return unchanged to the hand that threw it. This original vajra is a fitting metaphor for the empty clear knowing at the heart of Buddhist mystical practice, a non-conceptual illumination of experience that brings an end to reactivity and confusion yet is not impaired or weakened in the process.

The yana in Vajrayana means both path and vehicle — something that conveys you from one place to another. Here it refers to the teachings and practices through which you make the journey from ordinary consciousness to mystical knowing. Vajrayana, then, is a path or a vehicle that brings you to a knowing and experiencing of life undistorted by reactivity or confusion.

Other names for Vajrayana are Mantrayana, Tantrayana, and Secret Mantra. The Sanskrit word mantra means a magic spell and refers to spells that are used in magic and sorcery rituals. It also has a metaphorical meaning — that which protects the mind. In this context, it refers to the various methods used by mystics and magicians to protect their practice and their minds from distraction and disturbance. The word tantra is derived from the word for weft, the continuous thread that weaves back and forth as a carpet or a piece of cloth is woven on a loom. Tantra refers to a continuous thread of awareness, an empty clear knowing, that runs through all human experience. The term secret has two meanings. First, it refers to a way of knowing that is not accessible to ordinary consciousness. Second, it signifies that these instructions and practices are given only to those who are suitable.

Chapter Outline

In the Japanese film *After Life*, a group of recently deceased people find themselves in a lodge, in what turns out to be a kind of limbo. Other people are there to assist them to move on. These assistants ask them to go back over their life and choose the one memory that was most meaningful to them, the one they wish to retain for eternity. The genius of the film is that the recently deceased do not choose moments of triumph or accomplishment, but moments in which they were one with life. The assistants then reconstruct that memory in a film. As each person watches their film, something is completed and they move on.

In weaving this book together, I did not limit myself to one memory. What you find here are the understandings and the experiences that were most meaningful to me in my spiritual journey. The achronological order in which they are presented is intended to further your understanding of Vajrayana and to help you in your own journey.

Chapter 1 is about Vajrayana as a system of practice: its essence, its purpose, how that purpose is realized through practice, and the overall practice framework. The essence of Vajrayana is a clear empty knowing, a way of experiencing life in which awareness and experience are not separated. The purpose of Vajrayana practice is to bring about and stabilize shifts into that knowing. Because Vajrayana evolved out of ancient traditions of magic and sorcery, it relies on teachers who reveal possibilities, deities who wield and confer powers, and protectors who open paths in the dark. The two principal kinds of practice in Vajrayana are: the path of method, in which you build skills and capabilities, and the path of release in which awareness unfolds. Both are necessary, and when practiced properly they reinforce each other. The chapter concludes with a discussion of *ngöndro* or groundwork, a set of practices that for many is their gateway into Vajrayana.

Chapter 2 is about teacher-union practice. The chapter opens with an example of a teacher-union practice that makes explicit how faith and devotion, prayer, the union of minds, and direct awareness practice are all connected. It is followed by an experiential description of what it means to say that the mind of the student joins with the mind of the teacher. The chapter goes on to discuss each of these topics separately: what faith and devotion are, what prayer is, how faith and prayer help you to mature spiritually, and how they open a door to such direct awareness practices as *mahamudra* and *dzogchen*.

The next four chapters are about deity practice. Deity practice includes a vast array of methods that evolved in a different culture and a different era, namely, the mystical traditions of medieval

India. They are complex practices, and many people have difficulty in understanding how to do them. The aim of these chapters is to clarify these methods and make them accessible.

Chapter 3 is about empowerment, the entrance into deity practice. It opens with a story from my teacher that illustrates how this method of practice works. It then takes the reader through an empowerment ritual, making explicit how understanding and experience unfold. The chapter ends with a discussion of ethics in Vajrayana.

Deity practice itself is usually presented in two stages or phases, creation phase and completion phase. Creation phase is about becoming the deity and transforming the experience of life. Completion phase is about letting go of being the deity and transforming the experience of death.

Chapters 4 and 5 cover creation phase practice. In these two chapters your guide is White Tara, a peaceful deity associated with compassion, healing, and longevity. Moving step by step through a traditional practice text for White Tara, you experience the basic elements of creation phase practice, their connection with older rituals of magic, and how they purify or change your relationship with life. In Chapter 4 you take birth as White Tara in her world, her domain of awakening. In Chapter 5, White Tara comes alive in you. As White Tara, you mature into your powers, draw in the inspiration and energy of awakening, and draw on them to free beings from the vicissitudes of samsara. The chapter closes with your death as White Tara, and how you engage the intermediate period between death and birth that is, in the context of deity meditation, your ordinary human life.

Chapter 6 introduces you to a mediated completion phase practice called magical apparition, a practice from the Shangpa Kagyu tradition of Tibetan Buddhism. Here you learn what it means to die as a deity. In this chapter, you take three different paths into the experience of life as a magical apparition, one based on devotion, another based on intention, and the last based on transformation. All these approaches involve the transformation of energy. Because energy practices are inherently dangerous, this chapter concludes with general guidelines for working with energy.

Chapter 7 is about protector practice and balance. Here your guide is the Six-Armed Mahakala, the principal protector in the Shangpa tradition and an important protector in other traditions. A short daily offering ritual for Mahakala takes you through the essential elements of protector practice — ritual, sacrifice, and submission — and how these elements help you to maintain balance in spiritual practice. The chapter concludes with a second ritual, a burnt-offering ritual, that also helps to balance the forces that cause problems in spiritual practice.

Chapter 8 is about living practice. This chapter opens with instances from my own life when I was able to live the practice. Even though higher levels of practice are often described as no meditation, no practice, or nothing to train, actual living practice requires a high level of proficiency in a wide range of practices including mindfulness, awakening mind, taking and sending, creation and completion phase, and direct awareness. The chapter concludes with short summaries of the key points on which I rely to develop and maintain this level of proficiency.

Context and Structure

Though the last to be written, this book is the second in a trilogy on the practice of Buddhism in the Tibetan tradition. It assumes a knowledge and familiarity with Mahayana Buddhism as it is presented in the Tibetan tradition and how it might be practiced in today's world. This is precisely the subject matter of the first book in the trilogy, *Reflections on Silver River*, a translation and commentary of Tokmé Zongpo's *The 37 Practices of a Bodhisattva*. The present book, *The Magic of Vajrayana*, draws on several practice texts, each of them presenting a different method of practice. Together, they take you through the mountains and valleys of the profound purification practices of Vajrayana. The third book, *A Trackless Path*, is a celebration of the non-practice practice of dzogchen. It draws on a poem by the Dzogchen mystic Jigmé Lingpa and introduces the reader to the vast expanses of timeless awareness.

The aim of this book is to give you an actual taste of Vajrayana. To do so, I relied on practices and texts from my own training. They include practice elements from both the first wave of translations (the Nyingma) and the second wave, notably the Shangpa and Karma Kagyu lineages. My hope is that you find these examples helpful in your own practice, whatever tradition you follow, whatever deity you engage in practice, whatever practice text you use.

The main body of this book is instruction based on my understanding and experience. To focus attention on practice and avoid digressions, notes on background and historical context are placed in chapter notes at the end of the book. In addition, for those already familiar with Vajrayana, I compiled a glossary of terms with alternative translations.

How to Read This Book

The approaches I suggest here are based on how my own practice evolved after I left the three-year retreat. It is how I practiced within the complexities of life in a major American city, and it is how I taught others to practice in the same context.

If you are new to Buddhism or new to Vajrayana, read the book straight through without consulting the chapter notes or glossary. I suggest you read only a few pages at a time to give yourself a chance to assimilate the ideas and the practices. If the book does speak to you, you will probably read it again, and that will be the time to consult the notes and glossary.

If you are already familiar with Vajrayana, I still suggest you read the book straight through at first. Find the sections that speak to you and study them. Where applicable, incorporate the instructions into your own practices. In a second reading, spend additional time with the sections that speak to you, consult the notes, and apply what resonates with you to your own practice.

Conclusion

This book is about my experience with the practices that I received from my teachers. While I often delved into the history of a practice or a tradition in order to understand it better, I never succumbed to the conceit that what I practiced or what I taught was what Buddha Shakyamuni taught over twenty-five hundred years ago.

Many of the instructions I received were unknown in the time of Buddha Shakyamuni. To my mind, that makes them no less valid. One aspect of Buddhism's genius is that the experience of contemporary masters has the same authority as that of the original texts, be they sutras or tantras. As a consequence, practices have been able to evolve over the centuries, refined through changing times and changing cultures by the experience of the mystics and masters of their day. This book is a small contribution to the refinement of these practices for our times and our culture.

I practiced what my teachers taught me, trusting their training and experience. That trust enabled me to let go enough to give the practices a chance to work on me, rather than me work on them. Even so, at some point I had to take what I had learned and forge a way without knowing where it might lead. Here, timing is crucial. Too soon, and you may not have enough understanding and experience. Too late, and you may have settled into a way of practice that does not serve you.

The masters of the past and the masters of today sought exactly what you and I are seeking: a way of freedom. Yet it is not a case of following exactly in their footsteps. Like the young prince who became Buddha Shakyamuni, a master shows us a path. Through studying and learning from such masters, you and I may also find a path. That is my wish for this book, and that is my wish for you.

CHAPTER I

What is Vajrayana?

W hat is life? Even if you have pondered this question before, take a moment right now and ask it again. What is life?

What happens? For a brief moment, thinking stops. You are quiet, clear, and aware—clearer, perhaps, than usual. And everything is okay, even if it is not. The moment does not last long. You start thinking again soon enough. Even so, you have glimpsed another possibility, another way of being. What is that?

In 2019 I visited a Tibetan teacher, Kilung Rinpoche, at his center on Whidbey Island, off the coast of Washington State. Sixteen years earlier I had participated in a three-week retreat he had taught. While we chatted over tea, I asked him, "What is the essence of Vajrayana?" He was silent for a moment, and then replied, in Tibetan, "Dag nang."

"Empty experience," I thought to myself, a way of experiencing life and all its possibilities that is empty of self and empty of the projections of thought and feeling. Empty does not mean everything disappears. It means that the gap between you and what you experience disappears. Such shifts may arise spontaneously in artistic endeavors, in athletics, or in personal relationships. For instance, a close friend tells you that she has been diagnosed with cancer and the prognosis is not good. She and you are just there—not one, but not two, either.

Vajrayana practice creates the conditions for these shifts through teacher-union, deity, energy circulation, energy transformation, and other practices. At first these shifts are usually fleeting and unstable. Part of the purpose of training is to build the capacity to experience such shifts, stay in them for more than a moment, and allow them to inform and direct your life. Part of the magic of Vajrayana is that many of the rituals replicate the circumstances in which such shifts occur. When you perform the ritual, you act out the shift, both literally and symbolically.

Empty experience both leads to and is the result of direct knowing, a radical shift in which experience and knowing are not separate. Here there is no mediation by the conceptual mind. To know compassion directly is to be compassion. To know emptiness directly is to be empty. Direct knowing changes how the whole mind-body system functions. This radical shift has many names. As the 14th century master Rangjung Dorje wrote in *Aspirations for Mahamudra*:

> Free from mental constructions, it is called The Great Seal.
> Free from extremes, it is called The Great Middle Way.
> Because everything is complete here, it is also called
> The Great Completion.
> May I gain the confidence that, in understanding one, I know
> them all.

At one time or another, each of these names was a kind of pointing-out instruction, a word or a phrase designed to evoke a shift in a student. Other names are *nirvana* because it is the end of struggle; *the fourth time* because there is no experience of past, present, or future; *timeless awareness* because it is an awareness that has no beginning or end; *naked awareness* because it is utter simplicity; *ordinary knowing* because it is just there; and so on. The different names reflect how different teachers experienced this shift. Whatever the name, whatever the shift, for those who experience it, it has great meaning. For many, even though they may not be able to name it or say anything about it, it is everything, and it becomes the axis around which their lives turn.

The Three Sources

In 2013 at a party in Toronto I fell into a conversation with a well-known Canadian artist. In reply to his questions about where I was from and what I was doing, I said, "I lived in Los Angeles for many years, but that phase of my life is over. Now I wander, going more or less where the wind takes me while I figure out what to do."

"Ah," he said, "I've been there many times myself. There are two steps you have to take. The first is that you have to stop. You have to stop everything."

"Okay," I said. "What's the second step?"

"You have to stay stopped. Your old life will try to pull you back. You have to stay stopped—long enough for another way to become clear."

Stay stopped? Different words, but I knew what he meant. Do nothing. Do absolutely nothing and let mind settle and become clear by itself. Whether he meant to or not, this artist had told me to let my future direction evolve not from a concern for happiness, wealth, fame, or respect, but from unconditioned knowing, mind itself, empty clarity—whatever you want to call it. In Buddhist terms, he was telling me to take refuge in The Three Jewels: Buddha as emptiness, Dharma as clarity, and Sangha as immediate experience.

In Vajrayana, the corresponding three principles are the Three Sources: Guru, Deity, and Protector. At one level, Guru is the empty clear knowing of mind itself, Deity is mind taking expression in spiritual qualities, and Protector is mind taking expression in experience and action. These three comprise a spectrum encompassing everything you experience, from the pure being of mind nature to how you live your life. At another level, Guru is your principal teacher, Deity your personal god, and Protector your personal guardian.

In Vajrayana, a guru is not an ordinary teacher. A guru has experienced a radical shift into direct knowing and has the ability to hold that knowing in a field of energy. A guru also has the ability to transmit—to elicit a spark of awakening in you, whether directly from mind to mind, through a gesture or ritual, or through instruction. This is transmission.

A meditation deity (*yidam* in Tibetan) is a god who is an expression of awakened mind (buddha). Vajrayana is described as the path of result. You identify directly with the result of practice—awakened mind—which arises in form as your yidam or personal deity. This is a god you honor with offerings and praise, a god you invoke to look after you and take care of you, a god who inspires you, a god you evoke through ritual and practice, a god through whom you connect with the spiritual qualities you aspire to, a god with whom you identify, a god you seek to become yourself. To render you ready for deity practice, you are introduced to your deity through four empowerments: the vase empowerment, the secret empowerment, the wisdom-awareness empowerment, and the word empowerment.

A protector is also a personal god, a god who watches over you, helps you stay on track, and lets you know when you are heading into problems. At one level, a protector is your own wakefulness pointing you to effective action in your life. The wrathful form of most protectors conveys the awful power and immediacy of wakefulness. Like deity practice, you build a relationship with your protector through practice—through prayer, ritual, offerings, and energy circulation.

As that relationship deepens, the immediacy of awareness becomes active in your life. Series of cues, for example, point out next steps and pitfalls. You notice something a little out of the ordinary. You look, you see the cue, you drop into empty experience, and your next course of action is right there. When you take the cue, the circumstances of your life increasingly support your practice, materially, emotionally, and spiritually. When you ignore the cue, the circumstances of your life may deteriorate until you do pay attention to what is happening to you, internally and externally.

A Taste of Vajrayana

Explanations go only so far. What is Vajrayana? Another way to answer this question is to give you an actual taste. The following scenarios describe possible practice experiences and the changes those experiences may make in your life. As you read them, let the feelings and imagery flow through you.

The teacher's touch

"What am I doing?" you ask yourself. "Here I am, chipping away at yet another hundred thousand repetitions. I still have a week left, and that should be just enough time to complete all the repetitions of the teacher-union prayer and finish ngöndro."

Finish ngöndro? You are not sure what that even means. You are making good progress, at least in terms of the numbers, but so what? In the last few days a nameless dread has taken over whenever you sit down to a practice session. You don't really know what you are doing or why.

You started down this path because you felt called to something beyond the ordinary experience of life. In the writings of several mystics you read about experiences and a relationship with life that struck a chord in you. You knew nothing about meditation, but the Tibetan tradition of Buddhism seemed to be one of the few intact traditions of mysticism left in the world. You found a teacher and he told you to do this set of practices. But why?

One of the prayers reads:

Without thought of known, knowing, or knower,
Or ending of veiled, veiling, or veil,
A shift beyond goal, going, and goer...

Whenever you read these lines, a deep longing wells up in you. What you wouldn't give for a moment, a single moment, of clear pure being! But you don't see the connection between saying a prayer to your teacher thousands and thousands of times and the shift described in these lines. Still, you committed to completing this set of practices, and here you are.

Despite the nameless dread, you sit down and let your body and mind settle. You read through the opening prayers, including a long prayer praising every teacher in a lineage that goes back over a thousand years. You feel your teacher's presence right above you as best you can. You dig up the little faith and devotion left inside you, and start repeating the main prayer, counting each repetition on the rosary you hold in your left hand.

> Treasured teacher, I pray to you.
> Give me energy to let belief in self fall away.
> Give me energy to see through life's illusions.
> Give me energy to let reactive thinking end.
> Give me energy to know mind has no beginning.
> Give me energy to let confusion resolve itself.
> Give me energy to know that life is empty presence.

How many thousands of times have you said this prayer? While it puts words to what you yearn for, at the other end no one is listening. What have you to show for the hours and days of sitting and praying other than sore knees, a mass of confusion, and waves of frustration? All your faith and confidence are gone. An empty shell, you say the prayer. Why, you do not know.

You think about the words of the prayer, and your heart again stirs. To be free of self, to see through life's illusions, to know mind has no beginning—yes, this is what you want. Part of you says keep going. Another part says give up. Pulled this way and that, you don't know what to do. Through it all, you recite the prayer. By the end of the practice session you are worn-out and exhausted.

You return to the liturgy and read the concluding lines. You feel the presence of your teacher dissolving into light and coming into your heart—like water pouring into water, as the text says—and you rest. You like this part of the meditation session—no more praying, no more trying to feel faith or devotion, no more images or symbols to focus on. Your frustration and despair gradually subside. You sit there, relieved that another meditation session is almost done and a little sad because any understanding seems to be beyond your grasp.

As you sit there, a peace opens inside you. It is an unfamiliar peace, a peace you have not experienced before. You sit, letting mind and body steep in it. A slight shift and you enter a startling clarity. There are no thoughts. No, that's not quite right. There are thoughts, there and then not there, like snowflakes landing on a hot stone. They come and go in a vastness that has no measure, no dimension, no reference point. "What is this?" you wonder, but you are soon lost in thinking. You stop trying to understand and just rest. And there it is again, snowflakes on a hot stone in infinite clear space, a bottomless peace for which you have no words. How long you rest there you have no idea. Something moves inside you, you read the last verses and the dedication prayers, stand up and stretch, and go for a walk.

The world has not changed. Trees are still trees. Majestic branches sway in the same wind that sends waves through tall grass in the fields around you. A deep blue sky is studded with white clouds. The sun shines high above you. Another sun — your mind — blazes inside you with a clarity so intense that it almost hurts. What to make of all this you do not know, but a mixture of devotion, gratitude, clarity, and peace permeates your whole being and everything you experience.

Deity dreams

One day you wake up on a small grassy island in the middle of a large lake. You are sitting at ease, clear and almost weightless, as if your body were made of light. The dense jungle on the distant shores of the lake echoes with the sounds of eight white elephants roaming through the trees. Their crashing and trumpeting do not trouble you. The peace in you is so profound that you have no sense of time. Eventually you lie down, mind and heart utterly clear, and you go to sleep.

You wake up in your own bed, but the clarity and peace you experienced are still with you. Nothing has changed. Nothing is out of place. You brush your teeth, shower, dress and go to work. The peace and clarity come with you. The usual difficulties and inconveniences don't trouble or irritate you. You do your work, talk with colleagues, go to meetings, take notes, just as before, but the peace and clarity are always there. From time to time, you wonder if that day on the grassy island (was it really a day?) was a dream. It doesn't seem so. It was vivid and real, and the peace you experienced has stayed with you.

◇◇◇

Again, you wake up, this time in the center of a huge room. It is the main hall of an even larger palace built with marble floors and rainbow walls. Through the open doors you see a magnificent lawn, the verdant grass almost velvet in its texture. You see tall and stately trees from whose leaves you hear whisperings of strange and profound teachings. Herons, egrets, and peacocks stroll on the grass. You hear the melodies of nightingales, cuckoos, wrens, and other songbirds in the trees, and you see swallows and hummingbirds flitting through the air. Here and there you glimpse ponds, pools, and fountains with water of such brilliant clarity that it takes your breath away.

You look at your own body. It is green — a deep, deep green! You are seated on a brilliant disk, silvery white, like a full moon. You realize you are a woman, a maiden in the prime of her youth, and you are clad in loose flowing silks and gold jewelry studded with diamonds, rubies, sapphires, topaz, and emeralds. You are sitting completely at peace, your right leg slightly extended, the left drawn in. You hold the stem of a lotus in your left hand, its flower unfolding by your left ear. Your right hand rests on your right knee, the palm open and facing outwards in a gesture of generosity.

In this royal setting you are aware of the struggles and turmoil of beings all through the universe, some consumed by anger and envy, others by greed and desire, others by stupidity and pride. The moment your attention goes to them, your heart is filled with a compassion that cannot be put into words. You wish for them to know the joy, peace, clarity, and freedom you experience. Without thought or effort, your heart opens and light pours out, carrying with it thousands upon thousands of you in miniature form. They fly through space, touching the hearts of every being in every corner of the universe, instantly relieving their pains and struggles. You are the sun, the rain, and the earth, providing warmth, life, and nourishment. You bring peace, balance, joy, and understanding to every troubled being in every troubled world, without any thought or idea of helping or doing. You rest at peace, and in that peace you go to sleep.

You wake up. It is morning. You are in your own room. You look at your clock, and you see that a full day has passed. What happened? A sense of wonder lingers in the air, or is the wonder in you? Was that a dream? The peace you felt is still with you. You go about your day. Whenever you see someone having a hard time, the same compassion floods your heart. Whenever someone is unpleasant, dishonest, or deceptive, you also see their pain, anger, or fear. How you do not know, but the right words come to you, as if someone else is talking. You want to protect them from their own emotional reactions, but you know that all you can do is inspire in them a bit of the peace and freedom that permeates your being. At the end of the day, you go home, tend to your family, and go to sleep.

◇◇◇

When you wake up, you aren't sure what is happening. The joy of sexual union floods your being. Who are you? What are you? You seem to be simultaneously male and female, blue and red, embracing and being embraced—two but not two, one but not one. Energy flows through your whole being, from your very core to whoever or whatever you are and beyond. The bliss is like nothing you have experienced before. You have no words for it. There is no grasping, no tension, no wanting. It is full and empty, complete and nothing, awareness and space, all at the same time. An intense joy pervades your being with a peace and freedom that defy description.

You wake up. Once again, you are in your own bed in your own home. You have no idea what happened, but you feel the intensity of that joy—quiet, deep, pervading every part of you and everything you experience. The world appears to you like a dream, a mirage, a phantom. As you go about your day, you know exactly what to do or say, but that knowing arises free from thought and emotion. When you engage with people you are charming, firm, and direct; unpredictable, tough, and intimidating; and calm, understanding, and persuasive. Moment to moment, you embrace these possibilities with a deep, quiet energy and an equally profound and powerful stillness.

Protector power

You wake up in a charnel ground. Corpses lie around you, some bloated with putrefaction, others just skin and bones, and some fresh with raw flesh exposed by the ravages of wild dogs and vultures, covered now with hordes of flies. The stench is overpowering. You must be dreaming, but you are not sure. Afraid and uncertain, you look around and see a mass of fire blazing in front of a large tree. The scent of sandalwood fills the air. Curious, you take a few steps forward.

In the center of the fire is a figure blacker than the darkest night. Two feet trample on a white elephant, forcing a cascade of brilliant gems out of its mouth. Six arms slash the air above you with weapons. Snakes writhe around huge arms and legs. Clad in a tiger-skin skirt and an elephant-hide dripping with blood, he strikes terror in you with his frightening howls and deafening roars. Long canines protrude from his curled lips. Flaming hair and flaming eyebrows frame his dark visage. Three bloodshot eyes blazing with incomprehensible wrath bore into you, freezing you where you stand. Like the breath of a lion or a tiger, his energy hits you with a palpable force. You cannot move. Deep inside you, dark forces begin to stir. You feel your whole psyche shattering, crumbling, and disintegrating. And then nothing.

You wake up. It's morning. What was that? A dream, a nightmare, a vision, a visitation? You don't know. You decide to let it be, whatever it was. The memory gradually fades, but it never quite disappears. And something has changed in you.

Difficult situations are no longer as difficult. Sometimes a few kind words turn things around. Sometimes it takes a bit more — an apology, a cup of coffee, or a helping hand when it is least expected. At other times you stand your ground without threat or coercion, and let the difficulties resolve themselves around you. And in some situations, you bring an end to whatever is going on, firmly and decisively, without cruelty or thought of revenge. Where those capabilities came from you are not sure, but they seem to be connected in some way to that towering figure standing in that mass of flame in front of that enormous tree in that terrifying charnel ground.

Two Paths

In the second year of the three-year retreat we practiced a different deity every three months. We studied the practice texts, poured over commentaries, and peppered our retreat director with questions. We assembled whole worlds in our minds, but they kept falling apart. We became multiple deities in multiple mandalas until we didn't know who we were. We chanted mantras for hours, but we never met the expected numbers. We learned and performed monthly rituals, frequently losing our way as the ritual wove back and forth through different texts. And because each of us reacted differently to each deity, we were never sure how we, or anyone else, would react to the inevitable ups and downs in our regular routine.

When we started on the practice of the last of these deities, one of my fellow retreatants had had it. He could not bring himself to learn yet another practice and form yet another relationship with yet another deity. In each meditation session he read through the practice text, closed the book, and sat. When the meditation period was over, he opened the practice text and read the closing prayers. Over those three months he did none of the meditations or mantra recitations. Later he told us that of all the deities we practiced, he felt the deepest connection with that one.

There is a time to push and there is a time to rest. This principle takes expression in Vajrayana as the two paths, the path of method and the path of release.

The same principle is implicit in Buddha Shakyamuni's awakening. Tibetan paintings portray Mara's army of demons attacking

Buddha with all manner of weapons — knives, clubs, spears, planets, stars, and whole world systems. Buddha rests so deeply in this storm of reactive patterns that the downpour of weapons becomes a rain of flowers.

The ability to rest that way does not come easily. As a prince, he abandoned spouse, family, wealth, and position. He trained for years under the leading meditation teachers of his day. Then he undertook the most rigorous ascetism imaginable, eating one sesame seed and taking one drop of water each day. After seven years, he was so weak that he could not continue. His emaciated body had lost all its strength. His resolute mind had become cloudy and confused. He took food to nourish his body and restore his health, and his mind became clear and still. He sat down under a fig tree and rested in attention, letting things unfold on their own. Although traditional accounts tend to downplay his training, it was precisely his training that enabled him to rest, clear and present, as deeply conditioned reactive patterns rose up, raged, and fell apart.

In Vajrayana, the path of method is how you build skills and capabilities. In the creation phase of deity practice, you train to experience yourself as the deity. In doing so, you build skills in attention and imagination and you purify your life of all investment of self. In the mediated completion phase, you work with energy, directly or indirectly. You transform the basic energies of the body to experience bliss, clarity, and non-thought — familiarizing your mind and body with the experience of awakening.

By contrast, in the path of release, you let reactive patterns unfold and release on their own. Here is what the 11th century mystic Tilopa had to say:

Don't recall.
Don't imagine.
Don't dwell.
Don't examine.

Don't control.

Rest.

In other words, do nothing. Take a moment right now and do nothing. What happens? At first, nothing. But then you start thinking about what somebody said yesterday. You let that go, and you are soon thinking about what you are going to say tomorrow. You let that go, and you start thinking about your family. You let that go, but you try to figure out where thoughts come from. Fed up with thinking, you decide to stop thinking, but thoughts keep coming anyway. It's not so easy to do nothing! To do nothing requires skills and capabilities, skills and capabilities that you develop in the path of method.

Practice is a bit like riding a bicycle. When you have learned how to ride, you don't think about balance. You just ride. Body and mind make the adjustments on their own. You think about balancing only when you are learning. Thinking doesn't help much — it's too slow. It's your body that learns to balance. It's much faster than thought and it makes the minute moment-to-moment adjustments that prevent you from falling.

Deity practice is similar. By assuming the deity's form with all its attributes, you learn to hold an open field of attention. One of the results of that effort is a skill in balanced attention. Call to mind what happens when you are angry, or jealous, or greedy. Usually, you fall into some kind of story. If you are able to, stay in the reaction for a few moments and touch its emotional core. It is hard to stay there. Its intensity overwhelms you. One of the results of the energy transformation practices in completion phase is the ability to experience those emotional cores and not fall into reaction.

Unless you are extremely talented, path of release practice on its own does not go very far. Without balancing skills, energy abilities, and other capabilities, most people's practice of the path of release remains at a conceptual level. Milarepa, perhaps the most well-known of Tibet's mountain hermits, ran into this problem. Swindled out of his inheritance, he used sorcery to murder the swindler and his family, thirty-seven people in all. Regretting what he had done, he sought out a Dzogchen teacher who gave him instruction in a practice called Buddhahood Without Meditation. Milarepa did as instructed. He sat and did nothing. And nothing happened. Fortunately, his teacher saw that Milarepa was not ready for this practice and sent him to Marpa the Translator. For a long time Marpa refused to give him any instruction. Instead, he worked Milarepa to the bone, making him carry rocks and build and rebuild stone towers. Milarepa learned to hold his resolve and intention in the face of pain, despair, and hopelessness. The rest, as they say, is history.

Ideally, you practice both the path of method and the path of release. Because the efforts in each path are different, it is usually better to begin by practicing them one at a time. Most people do better by starting with the path of method. The skills and abilities so developed then make it possible to practice the path of release. As your experience with the path of release develops, you discover that you can practice the path of method while resting in the path of release. The path of release then enriches and deepens the path of method. Eventually the two paths come together. You practice mahamudra as the deity, for instance, or your deity becomes a door into timeless awareness.

A framework that helps to keep all this in perspective is to start every practice session with refuge and awakening mind, keep in touch with clear empty knowing while you practice, and end with a dedication of the goodness and understanding that come through practice.

Groundwork

In 1986 I organized a ten-day retreat with Kalu Rinpoche at Big Bear, a scenic resort area in the San Bernardino Mountains outside Los Angeles. About a hundred people attended. A couple of days into the retreat, Rinpoche opened the morning teaching with the following remarks. I was his translator.

"When Ken came to Los Angeles, he was very clever. He taught people to meditate on the breath. Many people liked this kind of meditation. It made them feel better. Many of you are here today because Ken taught this way. Ken is clever and he has done a good job teaching you."

Then, after a pause, he continued, "Maybe he is clever. But maybe he isn't so clever."

A ripple of nervous laughter spread through the hall. People glanced at me, puzzlement on their faces. What was going on? Was he teasing me? Where was he going?

"Maybe he is just afraid," he said. "Maybe he is afraid to tell people the truth, afraid of what would happen if he told them the truth, afraid they might run away."

Now the hall was dead silent.

"I'm not afraid," he continued, grinning from ear to ear. "I'm not afraid to tell you the truth, the truth about samsara, the truth about the workings of karma."

He then launched into an exposition of the struggles of the six kinds of beings, from the denizens in the hot and cold hells to the gods in the form and formless realms and everything in between, immediately followed by another exposition of how the workings of karma in endless cycles of birth and death stack the deck against any chance of happiness, let alone freedom.

His talk was based on the groundwork common to all the traditions of Tibetan Buddhism, four contemplations that turn the mind away from conventional concerns and toward spiritual practice. It left many of the people at the retreat a bit confused. Most of them had not heard these kinds of teachings. Was this the Tibetan Buddhist version of fire and brimstone? Or was it something else?

The four contemplations are the rare opportunity a human existence provides, death and impermanence, the workings of karma, and the shortcomings of samsara. In the afternoon classes at his monastery that Kalu Rinpoche held for Westerners, he drilled these four contemplations into us until we were sick of them, but he had a point. As I came face to face with the stark reality of my mortality, my priorities in life changed. I took to heart a Tibetan proverb about karma: "To see what you have done, look at what you experience now; to see what you will become, look at what you are doing now."

When I first arrived at Rinpoche's monastery in India in 1970, I could not relate to the meditations he taught. After several requests, he gave me the transmission and liturgy for the special groundwork practices. I had to learn enough Tibetan to translate the liturgy, and then I started. The first practice was taking refuge while doing full prostrations — 100,000 times. Combined with this practice was the practice of the bodhisattva vow, a short ritual in which I vowed to undertake the training of a bodhisattva in order to help free all beings from the vicissitudes of samsara. The third practice was purification. It included 100,000 repetitions of the long Vajrasattva mantra. The fourth practice was offering, 100,000 mandala offerings that symbolized offering everything beautiful in the whole universe. Finally, I did 100,000 repetitions of a prayer to my teacher, praying for his mind to join with mine. I did these practices, but I really didn't know what I was doing. Not only was I not familiar with meditation, the practices themselves were set in a cultural context that I was only just beginning to understand. I did each practice as well as I could until I had completed the count.

Three years later I was translating at Kalu Rinpoche's center in Vancouver. Inspired by my wife's example, I did the same set of practices a second time. I now had a much better understanding of these practices and how to do them. During Vajrasattva practice, I fell apart physically and emotionally, partially from stress and exhaustion from my work at the center, partially from the effects of the practice. Such coincidences are often regarded as a sign of purification, but it still took me months to recover. Then I worked through mandala offerings and completed the teacher-union practice. Nothing startling happened, but I felt I was preparing a solid foundation for practice, just as one would prepare a solid foundation before building a house.

Then a small group of us at the Vancouver center took to visiting Dezhung Rinpoche, a senior Sakya scholar and master, at his home in Seattle. A man of prodigious learning and tremendous warmth, he didn't think twice about taking an hour or more to answer even the simplest question. He told us stories about his own teacher Ngawang Legpa, a scholar and meditation master in the Sakya tradition. One story in particular struck me. At the age of 39, inspired by Milarepa's life story, Ngawang Legpa resigned from his role as the chief financial officer for his monastery and its estates and went to live in a cave above the main monastery. He lived there for fifteen years. Dezhung Rinpoche told us how Ngawang Legpa looked with longing at the lights of the monastery below him where the monks were warm and well fed. During those fifteen years, he did the traditional set of 100,000 prostrations 44 times, that is, 4,400,000 prostrations. The numbers meant little to him. He was taking refuge and cultivating awakening mind. Then he practiced Vajrasattva, a traditional purification practice. He did the traditional set of 100,000 repetitions of the 100-syllable mantra 21 times. Again, the numbers meant little. He was purifying his being.

That story changed my view of groundwork. Even though I had been told that the numbers were not that important, I still carried the idea of completing ngöndro. Ngawang Legpa's example, however, made it clear that groundwork is groundwork — it is done to establish a strong foundation. I then started a third set of the practices. During prostrations, I accepted the Three Jewels and the Three Sources as the guiding principles of my life. My connection with conventional life began to fray and fall apart. During Vajrasattva practice, I saw that good and evil have nothing to do with what I am — my first taste of what freedom might mean. I also saw how my own reactivity and confusion could put that freedom beyond reach. When I did mandala offering, I was brought face to face with my poverty-stricken attitude toward life. This time, mandala offering cracked open a door to the richness that life offers in each and every moment. For teacher-union practice I did a one-month retreat. It was an emotional and spiritual rollercoaster—periods of intense darkness and despair alternating with brilliant clarity, peace, and gratitude. I learned how powerful prayer can be, how it opens doors to inner depths. Only much later did I come to appreciate other doors it opened, doors into the practice of mahamudra.

It took three sets of groundwork practice for these understandings to put a dent in my emotional and social conditioning. Even so, I didn't feel any sense of accomplishment. The numbers were simply mile-markers on a longer journey.

When you are aiming to change your relationship with how you know and experience life, some form of groundwork is necessary. Metaphorically speaking, such a change is a pretty tall building and you need a correspondingly deep foundation. When my own students asked me about ngöndro, I made it clear that they would never be able to say that they had finished or completed it. They started with refuge (and prostrations). They did not count how many they did. They were given no timeframe or goal. It was their practice and they did it—for six months, a year, or possibly several years. Periodically, they checked in with me about their practice. For prostrations and each of the other practices, I looked for a specific shift in their understanding, experience, or motivation. When such a shift took place, I introduced them to the next practice.

While there are many aspects to the classical ngöndro that do not work well in a Western context, it was important for me in three ways. It helped me to understand what spiritual practice entailed. It developed skills, capabilities, and understandings. And it clarified, strengthened, and deepened my relationship with the calling that had started me on this path.

CHAPTER 2

Guru and Prayer

In 2008, I taught two retreats back-to-back at The Mandala Center in New Mexico. The center sits on the slope of an old shield volcano, opposite an old cone volcano. To the east are the prairies, to the west the foothills of the Rockies. Then there is the sky. I'm not sure why, but the sky seems bigger in some places than others. At this retreat center, the sky is very big, an expanse that evokes the vastness of direct awareness. The first retreat was on mahamudra, a direct awareness practice common to all the Kagyu traditions. The second retreat was on dzogchen, a direct awareness practice associated primarily with the Nyingma tradition.

After the first retreat, one of the retreatants asked me to compose a practice based on Niguma, an 11th century Indian mystic and the progenitor of the mahamudra teachings I had just taught.

Niguma's principal Tibetan student was Khyungpo Naljor (Tib. *khyung po rnal 'byor*), the mystic of the Eagle Clan. Born in Western Tibet in 978 CE, he was raised in the Bön tradition. Like many people, he followed his family upbringing. His intelligence and spiritual talent led him to become a teacher in Bön at a young age. Because he was not able to resolve his spiritual questions, he turned to dzogchen. Even though his natural talent propelled him into a teaching role, his spiritual questions remained unresolved. Frustrated yet determined, he set his mind on India. He was on the point of leaving when his elderly parents implored him to stay and take care of them. What could he do? He stayed, and continued his studies, practicing mahamudra first with one teacher and then with another — again to no avail.

A faithful son, he took care of his parents until they died. Then, at long last, he set out for India. The long and perilous trek from the high plateaus of Tibet to the steaming jungles of India is a difficult journey for anyone, but even more so for a man of fifty-seven years. He reached India, travelled widely, and studied with over a hundred and fifty teachers. Still, he could not find what he was looking for. Then he heard the name Niguma.

Khyungpo Naljor's meeting with Niguma has always inspired me, describing as it does the culmination of a long and difficult spiritual quest. The practice text I composed is based on this meeting. It is called *The Magic of Faith*. Let me take you through this practice, adding instruction and guidance at various points. You will find the whole text itself in the appendices.

FROM THE PRACTICE TEXT:

In the sky in front of me is my teacher, appearing as Niguma.

Every part of me, physical, emotional, mental, and spiritual, prays to her to be free from samsara's struggles:

I and all beings, infinite in number,
take refuge in Buddha, Dharma, and Sangha.
I and all beings, infinite in number,
take refuge in the teacher, in practice, and in what arises
        in experience.
I and all beings, infinite in number,
take refuge in experience, empty, vivid, immediate.

Repeat three times.

INSTRUCTION:

Let the figure of Niguma appear in the sky in front of you. Feel that she is your teacher appearing to you in the form of Niguma. She is not only your teacher. She is all of the teachers you have had or ever will have. She is all of the buddhas of the past, present, and future, all of the teachings of the past, present, and future, and all of the people in the past, present, and future who undertake a journey similar to yours.

Refuge is about the direction you have chosen to take in your life. Pray to Niguma as an example of what is possible, as the practice you do to bring that about, and as what arises in your life that shows you what helps or hinders you in your journey.

Also take refuge in experience itself. To take refuge in experience is to dispel confusion, reactivity, and conditioning. Confusion is dispelled by knowing directly, without recourse to the conceptual mind, that experience is your mind. Reactivity is dispelled by knowing that whatever experience does arise is movement in mind. Conditioning is dispelled by knowing that whatever the movement, it comes and goes on its own.

As you take refuge, feel that you are taking refuge with all beings, including everyone in your life—your parents and family members, your friends and colleagues, and especially the people with whom you have issues.

FROM THE PRACTICE TEXT:

> Beings are numberless: I vow to free them all.
> Reactions are endless: I vow to release them all.
> Doors to experience are infinite: I vow to enter them all.
> Ways of awakening are limitless: I vow to know them all.

Repeat three times.

INSTRUCTION:

Then turn to awakening mind. Where refuge is about direction, awakening mind is about commitment. Let the poetry of these lines speak to you as they take you deeper and deeper into the bodhisattva path.

Beings are numberless, and yet you undertake to free them all. However impossible, isn't that something worth striving for? Wouldn't that be wonderful?

Reactions are endless, yet you vow to release them all. What would that be like? Peace? Clarity? Freedom? Isn't that exactly what you are seeking?

Every time a reaction lets go, a door opens to a deeper experience of life. Here there is real joy. There is no end to the depths you can go.

And every door you enter brings a new dimension to awakening, a constant unfolding of understanding and ability.

A Walk in Someone Else's Shoes

The Magic of Faith is based on Khyungpo Naljor's first meeting with Niguma. Like many practices in the Tibetan tradition, it uses metaphor as a path to direct knowing. In this practice you are invited to trace Khyungpo Naljor's steps in his search for mystical understanding. Do so not by thinking about what he did or experienced, but by putting yourself in his shoes and feeling what he felt, praying as he prayed, and trusting as he trusted.

FROM THE PRACTICE TEXT:

Here in this forest, in the middle of my life,
Trees close in: a darkening path awaits my feet.
Much have I learned, yet more I seek to know.
What sense does it make for me to turn back now?

INSTRUCTION:

You are in a forest. Look back the way you came. See the trees thinning out, the sun shining through the leaves, and a path beckoning to you to return. Then look forward. See older taller trees with thick trunks and leaves and branches so dense they shut out all the light. The path before you quickly disappears into the deepening gloom.

What lies ahead? You don't know. Are you just starting out? Or are you like Khyungpo Naljor—years of practice failing to illuminate what originally called you? In either case, you have a choice to make. Do you turn back to the life you know or go forward, into the dark?

To keep going is an act of faith. What is the basis for your faith? Even though he has not had the level of direct experience he seeks, Khyungpo Naljor's faith is based in part in reason. He trusts what he has learned. He trusts the possibility of awakening. It makes sense to him. Trust based in reason takes him forward, as he prays to the buddhas and bodhisattvas to show him a way. What takes you forward? Repeat this short prayer again and again as you hold this question in your heart.

Buddhas and bodhisattvas,
Wherever you may be,
Please help me to find a way.

FROM THE PRACTICE TEXT:

Though teachers assure me time and again
About what they feel I know and understand,
My heart still longs for what no words will serve.
What is there to do but trust this yearning and go on?

INSTRUCTION:

Reason alone is not enough. Take a moment now and feel what calls you to this path.

For Khyungpo Naljor, it was a deep longing in his heart. Many of Khyungpo Naljor's teachers assured him that he understood the teachings. He had been a recognized Dzogchen master in Tibet. One of his Mahamudra teachers had said to him, "You know everything that I know." When he took full monastic ordination from the abbot of Bodhgaya, the abbot's nose started to bleed. The abbot said, "I'm not worthy to be your teacher." All these assurances did nothing to quell the longing in Khyungpo Naljor's heart. He knew that his own questions had not been resolved.

What about you? Have you had similar assurances? They come in different forms. Maybe you feel that your practice is futile. "Just trust your practice and understanding will come," you are told. As the years pass, however, these words fall short and this assurance grows less and less reassuring. Maybe you have been told that you do have a good understanding, but do you feel it? Maybe you have been told that you have had this or that insight, but does it salve the ache in your heart? Maybe you have been told that you have reached this or that stage of practice, but does that mean anything to you? Whatever the assurances, do they resolve the compelling yet inexpressible yearning that calls you to this path?

At this point you have to engage a different kind of faith, a faith that comes from the longing you feel in your heart and from listening, really listening, to that longing. Take a moment now and listen. Listen to your body. Listen to your heart. Don't listen to thoughts or words. Listen to what lies beneath thoughts and words. Listen until you feel that yearning, in your body as much as in your heart. Then pray from there, praying like Khyungpo Naljor, praying to the buddhas and bodhisattvas to show you a way.

To listen this way is dangerous. It takes you further into the dark. As you listen to your heart and give voice to its yearning in your prayers, other voices whisper in the shadows, "Don't do this. Forget these dreams. Go. Go back. Go back to what you know." Like Khyungpo Naljor, you continue to pray. The voices start to plead with you, but you keep going. Then they entice you with the prospect of companionship, comfort, and convention. Then they admonish you, "Why are you turning your back on life? You are making a mistake. This is no way to live." Then they undermine you, "You are confused. You are not thinking clearly. Let us help you."

You are at a crucial juncture. From a conventional perspective you are making a mistake, but your heart is telling you to go into the unknown. What do you do? How do you decide? Don't think about the past. Don't think about the future. Just listen, and let your body, heart, and mind grow quiet. In that stillness, what does your heart tell you? If the direction is forward into the dark, then follow in Khyungpo Naljor's footsteps. Pray again, listen to your heart, feel the yearning there, and trust what it tells you.

Buddhas and bodhisattvas,
Wherever you may be,
Please help me to find a way.

FROM THE PRACTICE TEXT:

"Find Niguma," I'm told. With the magic of that name
I find a strength that gently leads me on.
Dark the way, yet clear my heart and mind.
How does this mystery show me where to go?

INSTRUCTION:

There is a light in the dark, the light of your own knowing. Sometimes it needs a spark for you to recognize it. For Khyungpo Naljor, the spark is Niguma's name. What is it for you? A chance encounter? A snippet of conversation you overhear in a restaurant while having dinner with a friend? A book falling open at a passage you didn't notice before? A raven landing and looking at you in a way you cannot ignore? Whatever it is, you know what you need to do. You cannot shrug it off. You have no idea where it will take you, but you know you have to follow it. Reason and yearning are still there, but now there is a clarity, a knowing. Like Khyungpo Naljor, again you pray, but now you are led by a clarity that fills your heart and mind.

You are not out of the woods yet, literally or figuratively. You are still in the dark. It may be utterly dark, but there is a felt sense of a direction, a way to go. Do you know where it leads? Do you know what's ahead? No, you have no idea. All you know is that right now this is the way. Again, take up this prayer:

Buddhas and bodhisattvas,
Wherever you may be,
Please help me to find a way.

The skeletons of my life are scattered all about.
So is the rotting flesh of love and hate and fear,
And hair, the wild, wild hair of thought, wafts everywhere:
Oh, Sosa Grove, what have you brought me to?

INSTRUCTION:

In the stillness and clarity of your mind and heart, your life takes on a different guise. What do you see? The dead and those that feed on the dead? Bloated bodies, half-eaten corpses, skeletons, and scattered bones? Vultures, buzzards, dogs, and other animals watching with wary eye as they peck, claw, and bite into rotting flesh? Strands of hair, whispers of thoughts, that entangle you every time you move? You are in a charnel ground, in Sosa Grove. What are you doing here? This place is for outcasts. It is for those on the margins of society. It is for those who leave their dead to rot or be eaten. It is also for those who come to plunder the dead.

What have you come to? Questions, questions, and more questions crash like waves, engulfing you as you try to still your shaking limbs and trembling heart. Whatever led you to go into the dark? Why did no one come with you? Why does no one, neither family nor friends, have any interest in what drew you to this journey? How is it that the people you know, the people you love, and even the people you hate all seem to be going through the motions of life — like skeletons, zombies, and vampires? How is it that all that mattered to you, all that you loved, hated, and feared, now seem like lifeless rotting corpses? Even your cherished sense of who you are feels like a patchwork of memories and stories that held you together amid the unplanned, unpredictable twists and turns of life. Stunned and confused, you stand in the wreckage.

You cannot go back. That would be a kind of death, condemning you to live as a ghost forever haunted by what you once yearned for. To go forward is another kind of death, a death to all you have known. Pray again. Reach out to what you do not know. What else is there to do?

> Buddhas and bodhisattvas,
> Wherever you may be,
> Please help me to find a way.

FROM THE PRACTICE TEXT:

> "What are you doing here?" a voice shouts from the sky,
> "This place isn't safe, especially for the likes of you.
> Begone, before my companions soon arrive,
> And feast on you, your flesh, and, yes, your bones."

> Niguma!

> Dark tan your skin, black your hair, and
> Three eyes blazing like fire.
> The rattle of a drum in your right hand
> Summons your companions, intent and fierce.
> Your left holds a skull cup, and encircles Shiva's staff.
> At ease you sit as you turn your gaze on me.

INSTRUCTION:

How do you die to the life you have known? You look your fate in the face. For Khyungpo Naljor, fate is a half-naked, dark-skinned woman with a terrifying mien. She wears jewelry made from human skulls and bones, rattles a hand-drum, and holds a bowl made from a human skull. She glares at him, and tells him to leave before she and her companions devour him.

What is it like to face your fate? Does a darkness deeper than the darkest night loom before you? Do doubts and hesitations rise inside? Does your courage and resolve seep away? Do your knees shake and legs wobble? You chose to come here, but can you go forward, naked, alone, into the unknown? Khyungpo Naljor doesn't hesitate.

FROM THE PRACTICE TEXT:

> "Here, take this gold," I plead, "the last of all the wealth
>   I've known."
> "Is that all you have?" she sneers, tossing it all away.
> Grinning, her cannibal companions lick their lips with glee.
> For me what's left now? What more can I do?

INSTRUCTION:

The flesh-eating dakinis are licking their chops. They are ready to tear you apart as soon as you lose your resolve. Give. Give all you have. Anything less is not enough. Whatever you give, it is nothing in the eyes of your fate, but for you, it is and has to be everything.

Then pray. Pray for what you have always wanted. Pray for what you only now dare to put into words. Pray with an understanding, a yearning, and a clarity that cuts through all thought.

> Treasured teacher,
> In your presence I awaken free from time.
> I pray to you.
> For the sake of all beings,
> Give me energy to let belief in self fall away.
> Give me energy to see through life's illusions.
> Give me energy to master enchantment and dream.
> Give me energy to know the sheer clarity of being itself.

Pray to be infused with energy. Pray for your sense of self to fall away. Pray to see through the busyness and confusion of life. Pray to know that, whether awake or asleep, experience is experience. And pray to know the radiant clarity of being itself. Pray for your mind and heart to join with your teacher's, with Niguma's. Pray until you lose all track of time and place.

FROM THE PRACTICE TEXT:

> She smiles and, as I feel her light touch,
> I slowly rise into the sky.
> When I look into her deep black eyes,
> I meet space — open, vast, beyond all measure.

INSTRUCTION:

Some time later, you feel a gentle touch. You look up, and Niguma is right in front of you. You look into her eyes and you meet the vastness of the universe and beyond. You are no longer afraid. You are completely at peace. You hear her voice and her words ring like a silver bell:

FROM THE PRACTICE TEXT:

> Like and dislike are the mind's disease,
> Certain to drown you in samsara's seas.
> Know that there is nothing here at all,
> And then, my child, everything is gold.
>
> Experience arises like magic.
> If you practice like magic
> You awaken like magic
> Through the power of faith.

INSTRUCTION:

As she melts into light, her last instructions ring in your mind:

> Don't think about your teacher or your practice.
> Don't think about what is real or not real.

Don't think about anything at all.
Don't control what you experience.
Just rest in how you are right now.

With these words, she dissolves into light,
And, like water pouring into water,
She and I become one.

She dissolves into light. That light comes into you, and you rest.
You rest in a clarity and peace beyond words, beyond thought, beyond
understanding.

FROM THE PRACTICE TEXT:

I let go of all the good that comes from this practice:
May it touch everyone and everything I know.
May it ease the pain of struggle everywhere,
And awaken new possibilities for all.

INSTRUCTION:

Whenever you practice, you disengage from the endless stream of
confusion and reactivity that dictates much of what you do in your
life. Instead, you cultivate attention, compassion, faith, understanding, and other spiritual qualities. At the very least, when you practice,
you are not contributing to the chaos of the world. This is good. At
the end of every formal practice, take a moment and feel that goodness, and then give it a direction by making a wish that, in whatever
strange or mysterious way, it helps others by easing their struggles
or opening new possibilities in their lives.

◇◇◇

Why is teacher-union practice so important in Vajrayana? It is a big
question and it is best answered in pieces. What does it mean for your
mind to join with your teacher's mind? What is the role of faith and

devotion? What is the place of prayer? How does teacher-union practice lead to direct awareness, mahamudra, and freedom?

Joining with your teacher's mind

Consider the following analogy with music, though this same analogy holds with any other discipline.

You have been studying piano for some time. One day your teacher sits down and plays a piece of music for you, a piece you have never heard before. The music sends a shiver up your spine. You are frozen where you sit. You lose all sense of time. When she finishes, you are silent. You have no words.

At home, you try to play the piece as she played it, but something is missing. What is it? You try and you try. You recall so clearly how it sounded, how it felt. You recall how she sat and how she moved. You recall the phrasing and the subtle crescendos and diminuendos. Try as you may, however, you cannot make the music sound the way she did. You keep trying, for days, for weeks, for months, but it never happens.

Frustrated and discouraged, you cannot bring yourself to play another note. You give up and go outside. You walk and walk, down one street, up another, but her playing haunts you. Even though your whole being is bursting with frustration, you have to keep trying. You head home.

With trembling hands, you sit down and start to play. It is not right. You try again. It is still not right. You take a breath and let it out. Once more. Just once more. You recall that day in her studio. You see her clearly in your mind's eye. With tears trickling down your cheeks, you play the first notes. Something moves inside you. You are not moving your fingers. Something else is. You are not playing the music. Someone else is.

Music pours out of your fingers — but with a grace and lyricism all its own. Point and counterpoint, melody and harmony, it is all there. You play and play in an effortless joy, losing all track of time.

At some point you notice that you have stopped playing. Bewildered, exhilarated, exhausted, you have no understanding of what happened. Something did happen. You know it. You feel it in your body. And you know that you have changed, though you have no words to describe how.

The role of faith and devotion

In 1971 I met the Sixteenth Karmapa at his monastery near Rumtek in Sikkim. A person of extraordinary presence, he alternated between joyous laughter and intense seriousness with bewildering speed. As he talked with our small group, he stopped and looked right at me, his gaze penetrating to the very core of my being. "Your faith in Kalu Rinpoche must not change," he said, "whether you see him fly in the sky or kill a dog."

The penetrating power of his gaze has never left me. For years after, whenever I called it to mind, I felt a chill run up my spine. What he said, however, troubled me. Clearly, he was not talking about reason or rationality. Was he talking about blind faith, to accept unquestioningly whatever my teacher did? Or was he pointing to something else?

Many years later I was talking with a friend about faith and told him about this incident. His response was succinct. "It means that faith has to be unchanging and that it has to come from a place that doesn't involve reason or judgment." My friend is probably the last person to advocate blind faith. He, too, was pointing to something else.

In the early '90s, I participated in a small informal conference of Western and Asian teachers, Zen, Tibetan, and Theravada. At one point Gelek Rinpoche, a teacher in the Geluk tradition, said, "My teacher is buddha." Not *the buddha*, not *a buddha*, but *buddha*. He said it softly, his humility and reverence infusing his words with deep quiet power. It was clear that he was not talking about blind faith. He was not claiming infallibility or any other special qualities for his teacher. In his teacher Gelek Rinpoche had a human connection with a different way of knowing and experiencing life, a way that is at the heart of mystical practice. He had a human connection with buddha.

The faith or trust I have in my teacher takes expression as devotion — a combination of respect, appreciation, and gratitude. Devotion is not a belief or a posture that can be formulated in words. It is a feeling. It cannot be explained. It is just there.

"Was it always there?" you might ask. Not at the beginning. When I started to study with Kalu Rinpoche in India, I had been told only that he was a highly respected meditation teacher and one of the few willing to teach Westerners at that time. Nothing magical or remarkable happened when I first met him. I simply attended his classes, studied Tibetan, and practiced as best I could. As his translator, I came to appreciate and respect the range and depth of his knowledge and his abiding concern to point everyone he met in the direction of spiritual practice. I had little interest in the supposed miracles and signs that meant so much to other people. More moving for me were his struggles as a young man in the three-year retreat, how he slept leaning against the door so he would be woken up in the morning, or how he was perfectly happy meditating in the mountains, living on nothing but a bag of roasted barley flour through the winter.

My faith in him came primarily through prayer and practice, but I would be hard pressed to say precisely when faith turned into devotion, when devotion turned into commitment, or when I let go of a conventional life or career in Western society. When does a shoot become a sapling, or a sapling become a tree?

This is not to say that there were no tensions. There were. On one occasion I found myself stuck in a double bind, faced with the choice of a break in my relationship with my teacher or compromising my own values. Neither alternative was acceptable to me. I had to find another way. I had to look deeper. When I did, I found that the conflict came from my holding onto something that I was not aware of. I was seeing the situation only from my own cultural perspective. When I let go of that position, a way through the situation became clear, a way that maintained my relationship with Rinpoche and did not compromise my values.

Though wrenching and demanding, I made the same kind of effort when other tensions arose. Sometimes it was my attachment to my role as a teacher, or how I wanted the future to be, or what I thought was right versus what Rinpoche wanted me to do. In each case the tension between what my teacher was requiring and what rang true for me sent me deep into my patterns of reactivity and confusion. I learned to stay in that mess and experience it without trying to protect myself or anything I was holding onto, without trying to anticipate the outcome, without trying to control my fate. Only then did I find a way forward.

Karmapa's directive was in a way prophetic. Once it matured, my faith in Rinpoche never did change. When he died in 1989 I didn't feel any separation, and I never have.

Traditional teachings generally recommend that to deepen faith you recall the qualities of your teacher, of the teachings, of the Three Jewels, and so on. For me, that approach invites projection and idealization. Instead, when I practice teacher-union, I let my whole being steep in the experience of faith and devotion. I begin by feeling the devotion I have for Kalu Rinpoche — not just the emotional quality of that devotion, but the physical quality, too. Then I let my body, mind, and heart macerate in it. I rest in the feeling of faith and devotion itself, and let that work its magic.

When I practice this way, a deep quiet energy infuses me. Thoughts and feelings that would ordinarily have distracted me come and go like clouds in the sky. In effect, faith and devotion enable me to see and experience what arises from a higher perspective, a perspective in which hope, fear, and other deep emotional reactions are not destabilizing. They don't consume me and I don't need to suppress them. In fact, I don't have to do anything with them. I can let them be, and they take care of themselves. Through faith and devotion I discover the possibility of doing nothing in mind.

For me, there is a deep connection between faith and devotion on the one hand and direct awareness practices like mahamudra and dzogchen on the other. As you cultivate and nurture faith through practice and prayer, you form a relationship with a knowing that does not depend on the conceptual mind, a knowing that might be called a not-knowing. It does not depend on reason, deduction, induction, analysis, or inference. I don't know where it comes from, I don't know where it leads, and I don't know what it is. Yet it is there. I trust it, and that is all I can say.

Doing nothing in mind is the essence of mahamudra. Faith is one way into it.

The place of prayer

In the winter of 1972, I did a one-month retreat with my wife and another couple. We practiced four sessions a day, a routine broken only when we had to go to town for supplies.

My practice was Chenrezi—a deity that embodies awakened compassion. I couldn't do it. I couldn't visualize. I couldn't see myself as Chenrezi. My legs hurt. I was in constant pain. One day of misery followed another, all of them agonizing, confusing, and discouraging. Compassion for beings in the six realms of existence? I was in my own private hell, and I was not doing a very good job with it. Unable to do anything resembling meditation, I started to pray. My prayer was more an existential scream of pain and frustration than a coherent prayer, a scream combined with a desperate appeal to something, to anything, for help.

Prayer brought a little clarity and a little space into my confusion, and I found a way to continue. The whole experience was humbling—I did not and could not control what arose in my mind. Bit by bit, I learned that whatever did arise when I was meditating, I had to find a way to meet it, a way to be in it without losing myself in reaction and distraction. Often I couldn't. My attention was just not strong enough. Time and again, I was faced with a choice: I could fight with my mind until I was utterly exhausted, or I could acknowledge my inability, let go of meditation, and pray. In doing so, I kept a connection with the practice. I completed the retreat as planned, but more importantly, I learned how prayer and meditation work together.

Many teachers say that teacher-union practice is the heart of Vajrayana. In this practice, you pray. You pray to your teacher. You pray to your teacher as buddha. You pray for spiritual understanding. You pray for insights. And you pray for the ability to practice. Through prayer and through devotion to your teacher, your mind and your teacher's mind come together. A door opens, a door to the understandings, insights, and abilities you are praying for.

Treasured teacher, I pray to you.
Give me energy to let belief in self fall away.
Give me energy to see through life's illusions.
Give me energy to let reactive thinking end.
Give me energy to know mind has no beginning.
Give me energy to let confusion resolve itself.
Give me energy to know that life is empty presence.

This prayer has always spoken to me. I have said it literally hundreds of thousands of times. Even today, when I do teacher-union practice, this is the prayer I say. And just as I have done for decades, I go to the edge of the world as I know it and reach out. That, for me, is the essence of prayer: to go to the edge of what I know and reach out to the unknown. I pray to my teacher, but what I am reaching out to is more than a person. I am reaching out to what I yearn to know or experience, what is exemplified in my teacher—mind nature, direct awareness, whatever you want to call it. In reaching out I take a step towards that which is beyond what I know.

To reach out to the unknown can be terrifying. Individual experience varies widely, of course. In my case, I have to meet the unwillingness, mistrust, and raw fear that arise at the prospect of stepping into the unknown. From that winter retreat, I learned that I have to stand in all that, and experience it without being consumed by it.

The ability to do so, that quality of attention, does not come from the intellect or the rational mind. It comes from the heart, from faith, devotion, and trust.

When I reach out through prayer, the response is a deafening silence. In the face of that complete and utter silence, a maelstrom of reactions — anger, boredom, frustration, impatience, self-doubt, guilt, pride, and fear — erupts inside me. These reactions come and go, without rhyme or reason, and I have learned that those feelings are part of the practice of prayer. They return again and again at increasing levels of intensity. Why do I do keep coming back to such a practice? I keep coming back because it is what I am called to do.

Over time, through devotion, I have become increasingly able to experience all these feelings without falling into confusion. Even so, in this maelstrom, it is impossible to maintain any fixed idea of who or what I am. "I" feel abandoned, bereft, heartbroken, and lost. The two-edged sword of prayer cuts two ways. One edge cuts into the unknown. The other edge cuts into me and my confusion.

Sometimes, when prayer seems completely futile and hopeless, when there seems no point in tolerating the raging storms, the turmoil, or the confusion, there is an inexplicable shift — into a blazing clarity, a profound peace, or an inexpressible gratitude. These shifts come and go. In the next moment, I can plunge back into pitch-black darkness, despair, and intense mental and emotional confusion. Through all of this, however, a different kind of clarity begins to dawn — a clarity and knowing free from thought and movement, with no sense of inside or outside, clear and transparent, like space.

This way of praying leaves no traces. It acts like a fire, burning away confusion. When you reach out to what is unknown to you, you have to let go of the notion that you can control what you experience. You leave behind the conceptual mind and the mind of emotional reactions. The further you reach out, the further you see in, until you see absolutely nothing — the utter groundlessness of everything we experience.

Years later, when a group of students asked me for a contemporary refuge prayer, I drew on these experiences and wrote:

> Knowing there is nothing outside or inside to free me,
>> I take refuge in Buddha.
> Knowing that experience and awareness are not two,
>> I take refuge in Dharma.
> Knowing there is nothing to grasp or oppose,
>> I take refuge in Sangha.

A Way of Freedom

In 2003 I attended a three-week retreat in Colorado. My cabin was on a hillside that afforded a panoramic view of forested hills as far as the eye could see. A range of mountain peaks was just visible on the horizon. The silence was complete, highlighted by the songs of birds, the wind in the trees, rain and thunderstorms, and the grunts, scuffles, and calls of animals in the dark. The sun rose each morning, crossed the sky, and set, with the moon and stars dancing in the night.

In previous retreats I had usually followed a rigorous schedule of practices and rituals. This retreat was different. We met for one teaching session in the morning, one group practice session in the evening, and meals. The rest of the time was our own: no email, no cell phone, no text messages, no communication with the outside world, no practices to learn, no commentaries to study, no rituals. And only one meditation instruction. Do nothing.

Ajahn Chah of the Thai Forest tradition gives the following practice instruction:

> Put a chair in the middle of a room.
> Sit in the chair.
> See who comes to visit.

One has to be careful with such instructions in this day and age. Not everyone understands the poetry. A woman once came to see me and asked for a simple meditation instruction and I gave her this one. Later I learned that she did put a chair in the center of her living room, sat in it, and waited for people to visit. When nobody knocked on her door, she decided that meditation wasn't for her. I shook my head in disbelief when I heard this, but I had to acknowledge that in some ways I was like this woman. I would sit in what I thought was meditation, but I, too, was waiting for a visitor, a very particular visitor. I was waiting for something to happen.

In this retreat, however, there was no shortage of visitors. Relief, peace, a deep sense of relaxation, joy, and happiness were the first to come and pay their respects. "Ah, this is good," I thought, "let mind rest and it naturally becomes clear."

The visitors continued. The more deeply I rested, the more visitors came. They came out of rotting boxes I had stored decades ago in forgotten closets in mildewed basements — pleasant and unpleasant memories, stories about my life, old desires, impatience, frustration, boredom, and a sense of futility. I pushed them away but they kept coming. I analyzed them, but it made no difference. I tried to work through them, but that didn't help, either. I was back in an old struggle, trying to control my experience.

Day by day, my visitors became more disturbing, more demanding, more insistent. There was no way to keep them away. Some harbored hatred and a desire for revenge. Others cried with unfulfilled longing and yearning. Still others drugged me into a dull lethargy. They had no awareness of the beauty and peace around me, and no interest, either. They wanted my attention. That's all they cared about. And here I was, fending them off, struggling to find some peace and quiet, trying to reach my idea of a promised land. Do nothing? It seemed that I was busier than ever. I began to lose hope that I would achieve anything in this retreat.

Then it struck me. Hope was a visitor. Hoping was doing something. I had to let hope come and go on her own, just like all the others. The prospect seemed unimaginable. A chill crept up my spine and I found myself slipping into hope's counterpart, fear, fear of failure. I feared an acute disappointment if, at the end of the retreat, all

I had done was sit on a mountain and contemplated my navel. "Oh!" I thought, "fear is also a visitor." Bit by bit, I saw that to do nothing I had to let go of cherished hopes and subtle beliefs that I was just beginning to sense, including, in this case, the belief that I was at this retreat to achieve something.

Achievement, I found, was one of my more troublesome visitors. He poked his nose into everything! I am quite happy to do nothing for an hour or two, or, if I have had a particularly demanding stretch, a day or two. A few days at the most. But to do nothing, to produce nothing, to achieve nothing for a month, a year, six years, or more? That is a different kettle of fish.

I thought of my own teacher who had spent years in mountain retreats in Tibet. As he had told me himself, he would quite happily have stayed in the mountains. He left only because his teacher had told him in the strongest terms possible to return to the monastery and teach the three-year retreat. What was it like, I wondered, to be at peace with doing nothing day after day, month after month, year after year?

Then I thought about the 14th-century master Longchenpa, whose text was the basis for this retreat. He had spent fourteen years in a cave near Lhasa. What had it been like for him to do nothing day after day?

Here I was, practicing for a mere three weeks, worrying about whether I was going to achieve anything. The depth to which these teachers and many others like them had let go of any concern with success or failure was like a knife in my heart. Only then did I appreciate what letting go of hope, ambition, or achievement might mean, and I found myself feeling a different kind of respect and appreciation for those who had gone before.

Right from the beginning of the retreat, space surrounded and permeated my experience. Like my reactive patterns, I had largely ignored it. I had spent all my time and effort on trying to control unruly visitors, resolve emotional eruptions, and avoid old discomforts that lurked in the darker corners of my mind. Now I stopped ignoring this ever-present space and just stared into the sky. Whatever came up, I let it be there and tried not to do anything with it. As much as possible, I regarded those old ghosts as weather. Some days were sunny and clear. Others were cloudy and windy. Still others were stormy, with rain, thunder, and lightning. Movements arise in mind, but there is nothing to be done about them. They arise in awareness, but I didn't watch or observe them. I didn't try to resolve or fix them, and I didn't ignore them. Clouds in the sky, the teachings say, and I began to learn what this might mean, too.

Space, I realized, has many dimensions. In front of me was the vast space of the sky. It didn't depend on anything and nothing depended on it. I watched the play of light and colors as the day passed. When the sun set and the sky lit up with shades of rose and yellow and purple, the space that let me see the sunset didn't take on any color, yet it was not something apart. At night, it became an empty blackness, punctuated by a thousand points of light, but the panorama of stars was not separate from space.

Silence is another kind of space. When everything is quiet and suddenly a bird calls or a dog barks, we ordinarily say the silence was broken. But it is more accurate to say that our attention goes to the sound and we stop hearing the silence. I started to listen to the silence, around me and inside me, even when voices were chattering in my head.

Time is another dimension. Immanuel Kant once said that time is the medium in which we perceive thoughts, just as space is the medium in which we perceive objects. Hopes and fears, projections into the future, regrets, and joys are all thoughts that come and go in time. Because there was nothing to do with any of them, I began to experience them as comings and goings, like the mists that rose from the trees in the early morning, only to vanish as the day progressed. Some days, what arose was more of a thunderstorm, but, like the thunderstorms in the mountains, the thunder and lightning came and went on its own, leaving space as it was before, and the ground and trees refreshed and rich with life.

I became aware of another dimension, an infinite internal space that had to do with my body. This dimension had more the quality of depth: it seemed to go down forever. There was no bottom. There was no me there. It was like a bottomless abyss, except that sometimes, I was the abyss. Years later, when discussing this experience with an aging teacher, he said it was *zhi mé tsa tral* — a Tibetan phrase that means no ground, no root.

Like the woman in the chair who waited for someone to knock on her door, I had been waiting for something to happen, some experience or insight into a truth that made sense of everything, put all the ghosts to rest, and silenced the thousand voices in the dark. For decades, I had held the belief, deeply embedded in our culture, that freedom lies in knowing the truth. Slowly, it was becoming clear to me that there is no truth, not out there, not in me. There is only what we experience, and we have a choice between two different ways of meeting it.

The first is explanation. Explanations rest on deeply held assumptions that I may or may not be aware of. Even when I say that I am exploring my experience, I am usually looking for evidence that supports or confirms those assumptions. The assumptions themselves are not questioned. Nor do explanations put you in touch with actual experience. They keep experience at arm's length, as an object whose existence can be explained. Mystery is dismissed, every possible door to it shut and barred as soon as it appears. This is the prison of the conceptual mind.

The other way is to open and be willing to receive and not control what arises in experience, not explain it away. In this approach, my effort is not only to allow, but to embrace every sensation, feeling, and thought. It is to accept that much in life cannot be explained, it can only be experienced. It is to let experience challenge, expose, and uproot ideas and assumptions. It is to live life as it comes to me, and not seek understanding or explanation in fundamental or eternal truths. It is to live in not knowing.

Early in the retreat, when difficult experiences arose, I would analyze them, trying to understand what had happened and why. I thought understanding would help to resolve them and they would stop bothering me. It did sometimes, but not very often. Sometimes I would be completely swallowed by emotions and sensations and the stories they spun, and only come to my senses a few minutes, or a few hours, later. Frequently, I just could not face what was arising. I had to shut it down or go for a walk. Body movement often helped me to be in the raw experience. But most of the time, if what arose did not fit my picture of what I wanted or needed, I would start doing something.

When I became aware that doing something, doing anything, was a way of avoiding what I was experiencing, I began just to stare into space in any of its dimensions: the vast vault of the sky, the utter stillness of silence, the ungraspable mystery of time, and the infinite depth in my body. I learned that the only way I could do nothing was do nothing—receive whatever arose, experience it, and do nothing with it. I needed a certain capacity to experience powerful feelings such as loneliness, worthlessness, despair, or shame. When those visitors came, I let them be there, not reacting to them or pushing them away. It was hard and I often felt I like I was dying.

I recalled the many times Kalu Rinpoche had said to me, "Rest in just recognizing." No one had said, however, that "just recognizing" might lead to pain so intense that I would not wish it on my worst enemy. Even then, there was nothing to do but experience these feelings as best I could. I gradually came to understand that the potential to recognize what was arising and not do anything with it, no matter how blissful or painful it might be, is part of what we are. And I came to appreciate that I had the capacity to do so at least partly because of the years of training and practice I had done before this retreat.

As I continued to open and experience, I discovered that there is nothing to oppose. There is no enemy. Nor is there any absolute or ultimate truth, state of perfection, ideal, or final achievement. Such phrases as "all experience is empty" or "everything is an illusion" are better understood as descriptions of experiences, not statements about reality. Reality is beyond words. On the other hand, to be free of suffering, to be free of struggle, involves nothing more than to stop opposing what arises in experience: to practice in everything the simple dictum, "there is no enemy."

CHAPTER 3

Deity and Power

A successful business man, despite his fortunes, was dissatisfied with his life. Not knowing what to do, he paid a visit to a spiritual teacher he had known for many years.

"I have more wealth than I could possibly need. It does not bring me any peace, just as you have taught. Please tell me how I can find peace of mind."

The teacher said nothing for a few minutes. Then he looked down and scanned the ground around him. He picked up a small white stone, smooth and rounded. "Convert your wealth into white stones like this one," he said.

"All of it?" the man gasped.

The teacher nodded.

The man set about doing what the teacher had advised. He arranged with brokers to convert his tangible assets into cash. He talked with other brokers who found buyers for his companies. He contacted agents and asked them to find sources for white stones. He purchased a large tract of land to serve as a repository for his stones. Then he bought stones — mountains and mountains of white stones. He had to arrange for ships to carry them from all over the globe. He had to buy trucks and other machinery to unload the shipments and deposit them on his land. He was a capable businessman and a good organizer. Even so, it took him years to liquidate all his assets, find sources for white stones, arrange for their purchase, have them loaded and shipped, and, then, at their journey's end, have them unloaded and deposited in the repository.

When the last shipment arrived, he looked over the field of white stones shining in the sun — a field of brilliant white as far as the eye could see. "What a sight!" he thought. He felt a great wave of relief. Look at what he had accomplished! And he no longer had the burden of wealth, of companies, or of business deals. Still, there was some nagging residue. He was not completely at peace.

He returned to the teacher and described what he had done and what a joy it was to look over the field of white stones.

The teacher nodded, leaned forward, and whispered in his ear, "Who needs white stones?"

Deity Practice

Deity practice is a purification practice. It empties the way you experience life of any investment of self. You develop certain powers through this purification — in particular, the power to be aware in whatever arises. This power leads directly into the practice of direct awareness.

Deity practice begins with an empowerment ritual in which your teacher introduces you to a deity, your personal god. In this ritual, seeds of experience are planted in you. Through practice, these seeds grow and mature into actual empowerments — radical shifts that change how you know and experience life. Of the thousands of empowerments and deity practices in the Tibetan tradition, I have chosen Wishing Wheel — White Tara — to be your personal deity. This chapter takes you through the empowerment ritual. The two subsequent chapters take you through the practice.

You are waiting outside the hall where your teacher will perform the empowerment ritual. The door opens. An attendant holds a jeweled vase, a bit like a small Russian teapot. He pours a few drops of water into your cupped right hand. You take the water into your mouth, swish it around, and spit it into a bowl that has been set there for this purpose — a ritual ablution. You are about to enter a different world. Before you enter, you wash away everything you have done in thought, word, or deed to cause harm, shame, regret, or pain to others or to yourself.

You slip off your shoes and enter the hall. Your teacher is sitting on a throne. He wears formal robes. You bow three times, sit down, and join him in reciting the long Vajrasattva mantra, a mantra that clears away the karmic residues of reactivity and confusion.

He takes a baton decorated with peacock feathers from the vase of purification water and sprinkles a few drops on a small figurine made of flour and water. He chants a peace offering to any disruptive spirits present. "Please take this offering," he says, "and leave us alone." An attendant takes the figurine outside. Your teacher continues to chant, telling the disruptive spirits that he will destroy them if they do not leave. Then he rings his bell and rattles a hand-drum to punctuate his threat. He starts a different chant, sending out wrathful deities to destroy any negative spirits who do remain, waving in circles the vajra scepter he holds in his right hand to establish a protection circle, and strewing flower petals around the room to set the boundary. You have entered a different world, a world imbued and protected by magical and spiritual energy.

Your teacher places the vajra and hand-drum on the table in front him. "Why, exactly, am I taking this empowerment?" you ask yourself. The answer comes in the next words from your teacher.

"You take this empowerment in order to free all beings from their struggles in samsara. To free all beings, you become White Tara. To become White Tara, you do this practice. Hold this intention in your heart as you receive this empowerment."

Where does this empowerment come from? Again, in the words of your teacher, "Avalokiteshvara, Great Compassion, gazed over the whole universe and heard the groans of countless beings struggling in samsaric experience. Moved by their plight, he shed two tears. One became Green Tara, the other became White Tara, both expressions of the activity of compassion. The great Indian master Atisha had a special relationship with Tara, and he brought this practice to Tibet in the 11th century. For over a thousand years it has been transmitted from teacher to student. Today I give it to you."

You now make a symbolic offering of everything wonderful and beautiful in the whole universe. Then, with palms joined together, you formally request the empowerment itself. Through this ritual offering and request you give dramatic expression to two important points. With the offering of the universe you acknowledge to both your teacher and yourself that this practice, this opening of a way to mystical understanding, is more important to you than anything the world has to offer. Likewise, through the formal request, you are asking to be shown a path that may change your life. You are doing so of your own volition. You are doing so not only for yourself, but for all beings who struggle in their lives. In making this request, you assume responsibility—for doing this practice, for how it changes your life, and for how you help others.

Vajrayana, like all Mahayana practice, is based in awakening mind, the union of emptiness and compassion. To prepare for the actual empowerment, you pray with your teacher to renew your connection with awakening mind, your commitment to the bodhisattva vow, and your resolve to help all beings become free of samsara.

"All experience is naturally pure. You are naturally pure." Your teacher utters these words in Sanskrit, and the way you ordinarily experience life dissolves, like mist in the morning sun. Step by step, you follow your teacher's directions as if you are dreaming.

You are White Tara. Your body, clear and white like moon crystal, shines with the light of all the colors of the rainbow. Charming and attractive, you are graced with extraordinary beauty. Your smile radiates peace. You have three eyes on your face and one eye in the palm of each hand and the sole of each foot—the seven eyes of timeless awareness. Your right hand is extended in the gesture of supreme generosity. Your left holds at your heart a hundred-petalled white lotus, its stem held between the thumb and ring finger, the flower itself blossoming beside your left ear. You wear beautiful jewelry wrought of gold and set with pearls and other precious stones—a crown, earrings, a short necklace, a longer necklace, a string of jewels, bracelets and anklets, and a belt with tiny bells. You are decorated with heavenly flowers and wear a white silk blouse and a rainbow-colored silk skirt. Your jet-black hair is partially bound up. Your feet rest in vajra posture and you lean back against the full disk of the moon.

Tara also appears in front of you on the shrine, a mirror image of you — or are you a mirror image of her? Whichever the case, you know that you receive the empowerment from her.

You see your teacher, too, as White Tara. Brilliant light shines from her heart. The light elicits even more brilliant light from the shrine Tara. Light of every color of the spectrum shines from her whole body. A stream of light forms and flows into you through your forehead, cleansing you of every impurity, every illness, every lapse in attention, every emotional eruption, every shameful, hurtful, or mistaken action, and all associated karmic conditioning.

The shrine Tara again blazes with light, its effulgence illuminating the entire universe. The light draws in the power and energy of buddhas and bodhisattvas throughout all time and space. Their qualities and abilities, in body, speech, and mind, take form as White Taras, some as big as mountains, others as small as snowflakes. They pour into you from all directions, merging with you and investing you with the power, understanding, energy, and compassion of the primordial White Tara — the understanding and energy of timeless awareness. You become White Tara and rest in indescribable light, unfathomable emptiness, and inexpressible bliss.

Music fills your ears and the fragrance of saffron and frankincense wafts through the air. Something touches you on the top of your head. It is your teacher sealing this shift by making a cross on top of your head with the vajra scepter he or she holds.

Having prepared the ground with the experience of becoming White Tara, you again ask to be empowered in body, speech, and mind. Through a similar process of meditation combined with ritual action, you receive the empowerments of body, speech, mind, capabilities, and action.

Your teacher, as White Tara, calls on the empowering deities — the heads of the five buddhas, the five female buddhas, the six male bodhisattvas, the six female bodhisattvas, and the ten sentinels. They gather in the sky in front of you. The five female buddhas anoint you with elixir from the vases they hold. The clear shining elixir flows through you, instantly clearing away all karmic propensities for unwholesome actions, emotional eruptions, physical illness, and untimely death. Overflowing, the elixir swirls above your head, taking form as Amitabha Buddha, the Buddha of Infinite Light. At the same time, your teacher touches your forehead, throat, and heart with a vase from the shrine and pours a few drops of water on you. The energy of White Tara's form floods your body, and you know that you are now able to assume her form.

Then White Tara's mantra appears in your heart, brilliant white letters arranged above a white eight-spoked wheel. A similar arrangement appears in the heart of the White Tara in front of you and in the heart of your teacher as White Tara. As you repeat Tara's mantra, chains of mantras vibrating with the sound of her mantra arise from their hearts and come into yours, bringing the sound and energy of her mantra into your heart. As your teacher voices each syllable of Tara's mantra, you, too, repeat each syllable in turn. Then, calling on White Tara directly, your teacher asks her to protect you, to charge you with the power of her mantra, to sustain you in your efforts to awaken, and to make your understanding present in everything you do. The energy of White Tara's mantra fills your heart, and you know you are now able to invest whatever you say or recite with her energy and understanding.

Brilliant light shines from your teacher's heart, inviting the power, attainment, energy, and timeless awareness of all the teachers, meditation deities, buddhas, bodhisattvas, warriors and dakinis, and protectors and guardians in the ten directions. All these aspects of awakened knowing and experience take the form of white lotus flowers. They pour down on you like rain. As soon as they touch you, they dissolve into light, melting into your body and filling your heart. In your heart, White Tara's seed syllable, *tam*, radiates light that moves the mind and heart of the shrine Tara. From her, a second White Tara arises like a flame from a candle. This second Tara pauses right above your head, melts into light, and comes into your heart. Everything she knows and understands floods your whole being, filling your heart and mind with her energy. Your teacher then says:

> Let thoughts about the past, the present, and the future drop away. Just rest. Don't try to do anything. Rest deeply, open to what arises, and be that knowing in which awareness, clarity, and emptiness are not separate.

With these words, your teacher touches your heart with a white lotus, the mind of White Tara. With that touch, you know that you are now able to touch White Tara's mind in everything you experience.

Your teacher, in the form of White Tara, presents exquisite jewelry and silk clothes to you, also as White Tara — a crown, earrings, bracelets, anklets, and necklaces and a blouse, skirt, shawl, and scarf. She places them in your hands and drapes them over your form, saying:

> This is the fine silk and rich jewelry
> Of noble Tara.
> If you always hold onto it,
> You will come to embody
> The capabilities of all buddhas
> In the three times.

With these gifts gracing your form, you know you can work with the channels, energy, and vital essences to cultivate the unlimited capabilities of the path. Your teacher then touches your hands with a picture of jewelry and silk, and you bring that touch into your heart.

Both your teacher as White Tara and the shrine White Tara radiate light of five colors — white light from their foreheads, red light from their throats, blue light from their hearts, yellow light from their navels, and green light from their genitals. The light is a signal to buddhas and bodhisattvas in every realm. It draws in the power and energy of the four kinds of awakening activity — calming, enriching, magnetizing, and destroying — in the form of streams of light of each of the five colors. The white stream of light comes into your forehead, the red to your throat, the blue to your heart, the yellow to your navel, and the green to your genitals, filling you with power and energy.

White light shines from your forehead, filling the universe with its brilliance. It calms all illness and disease, emotional eruptions, harmful and hurtful activity, and all the confusion and reactivity that create pain and suffering in the world. Then yellow light shines from your navel. It brings nourishment and prosperity to every being, enriching and extending their lives, and increasing the good they do. Red light shines from your throat. It transmits power and energy to each and every being, enables them to stand in their natural dignity and subdue what is problematic and troublesome, and energizes them to realize their aims for both others and themselves. Blue light shines from your heart. It destroys the power and influence of the four demonic obsessions and frees all beings from the disruption and harm of confusion and reactivity. The green light from your genitals then permeates the whole universe, doing whatever needs to be done to free all beings from the confusion of samsara.

All this light, as well as the light from the buddhas and bodhisattvas, comes back into you. You hear your teacher say, "May you perform the infinite work of a vajra master, taking care of students in all the different ways." You look up, and your teacher's right hand is holding a vajra and the left a bell. You take these implements with the same hands and hold them crossed over your heart as your teacher says:

Hold the great vajra and great bell;
Be infused with the energy of the vajra.
Today, you become a vajra master.
Gather students around you.
Perform all appropriate actions.

With this final empowerment, you know that you now have the potential to do whatever it takes to bring all beings everywhere to full awakening.

To conclude the empowerment ritual, you make a promise of obedience, present offerings, and dedicate goodness.

Seeing your teacher as White Tara, you repeat the following promise three times:

I promise to do
All that my teacher tells me to do.

Having been anointed by the empowerment deities, you promise to obey White Tara, your teacher, through whom you received this empowerment and from whom you will receive instruction and guidance. You also make this promise in the presence of timeless awareness, that is, the White Tara who is the shrine deity.

Then, in an expression of gratitude, you present a second offering of the universe. As White Tara, you summon showers of gold, silver, jewels of every kind, cascades of fine silks and delicate cashmeres, exquisite melodies sung by the ethereal voices of heavenly choirs, clouds of frankincense, sandalwood, and other fragrances, tables of the finest foods of every description, fine beverages, and bouquets of flowers. These offerings rain down from the heavens, showering both your teacher as White Tara and the shrine White Tara with whole world systems filled with riches and beauty beyond description. To these, you add your personal offerings, which you place in front of your teacher.

Finally, you join with your teacher in the dedication of the goodness and understanding generated by the empowerment ritual. As White Tara, light streams from your body, illuminating every corner of the universe, touching each and every being with the goodness and understanding that have come to you today, instantly relieving their pain and struggles, and opening countless doors to their own awakening.

After this final dedication, you leave. You leave the physical space in which the empowerment ritual took place and you step out of the sacred and magical world in which it was given. Something has changed, but exactly what is hard to describe.

◇◇◇

Ideally, when you receive an empowerment, you have a vision of the deity, a palpable sense of the deity's presence, or a shift into empty experience. You may experience emptiness, clarity, bliss, non-conceptual compassion, or a heightened exhilaration, energy, devotion, or gratitude.

For the vast majority of empowerments that I have received, however, nothing special happened, and that seems to be the rule rather than the exception. Instead, I was left with more questions than answers. How have I been empowered? How do the seeds grow? What does the promise of obedience entail?

How have I been empowered?

In the empowerment ritual, there are several modes of transmission, any one of which plants a seed of experience. One is the ritual itself—the description of the deity, the vase anointment, repeating the mantra, the pointing to the deity's mind (the white lotus in the case of White Tara), and so on. At one level, this is all theatre. You participate in a drama in which you are introduced to White Tara and through which you receive her understanding, powers, and capabilities. In physically acting out each part of the empowerment, a seed of experience is planted in your body and in you.

Another mode of transmission is devotion. On many occasions, a teacher from whom I was receiving an empowerment would say, "Let devotion arise strongly. As you feel that devotion, feel that you are also receiving this empowerment." Then he or she gave the empowerment with little or no explanation. It was as if devotion opened a door through which some part of me could be touched by the presence of the teacher as the deity.

Another is energy. Before, during, and after the empowerment, a teacher holds a field of energy. More than a few of my fellow practitioners felt (and sometimes saw) that field, but that happened to me only occasionally. The energy field carries the spirit of the deity. As the energy permeates your body, heart, and mind, a seed of experience is planted.

Still another is the magic. Before you entered the hall to receive the empowerment, your teacher had already become White Tara and generated White Tara on the shrine. Then, using the power of mantra, your teacher had charged the vase used in the empowerment with the energy of White Tara. Your teacher then took exactly the same empowerment you receive, taking it from the shrine deity. After you entered, he or she cleared the space of all disruptive spirits, established a protection circle, and then gave you the empowerment. After you have left, your teacher makes offerings to White Tara and the empowerment deities, and then dissolves the whole assembly. This is magic — the use of intention, energy, and ritual to change what you experience.

Sometimes it is simply a matter of resonance. Something in you resonates with something in your teacher, the deity, or the ritual, and a seed is planted.

Teachers give empowerments in different ways. Some teachers provide clear guidance during the empowerment ceremony, explaining what is happening at each step, what you should be practicing, and what that step means. Others rely on the ritual itself, and give the empowerment with no explanation. Others generate a field of energy and trust the field of energy to plant the seed. Some teachers dispense with a formal ceremony and lead students through the practice of the deity, doing the practice with them. And some give an empowerment over a cup of coffee.

How do the seeds grow?

On more than one occasion I asked my teacher if I had actually received the empowerment, even though I had had no special experience. The answer was always an unambiguous yes. He went on to explain that a seed planted in an empowerment ritual would grow through practice, first into shifts in my understanding, then into shifts in the way I practiced, and finally into a transformative shift in the way I experienced life. That transformative shift was the actual empowerment, the ripening of the fruit that grew from the seed planted in the ritual.

For instance, in several empowerment rituals, I was shown a mirror, or a picture of a mirror, as a symbol of the mind of the deity. Initially, I interpreted the symbol conceptually — mind is clear and empty, like a mirror. One day it dawned on me that when I look at a mirror, I do not see the mirror. I see only reflections in the mirror. "Hmmm," I thought, "maybe, when I look at mind and all I see are thoughts and images, I'm actually looking at mind. Those thoughts and images are mind. They are not separate from mind in the same way that reflections are not separate from a mirror." That understanding changed how I practiced. I could look at a mirror, look and not see it, and look and not be distracted by the reflections in it. In the same way, I could look at mind and not see anything, yet rest in the looking undisturbed by the coming and going of thoughts. As attention grew more stable and clearer, I could look and see nothing, even when anger, jealousy, or desire churned in me. The same held true for other kinds of emotions, for loving kindness, compassion, all the immeasurables, and for faith and devotion, too. One day, more or less out of the blue, I suddenly understood that all experience is movement in mind, nothing more, and nothing less — an understanding that enabled me to drop into clear empty knowing with a slight shift in attention.

What does the promise of obedience entail?

An empowerment ritual is theatre, a play in which every aspect is freighted with spiritual significance. At the end of the White Tara empowerment, at the end of the play, you promise to obey your teacher. This promise is part of the play. It is not a literal promise — it is deeper than that, much deeper. It is a sacred promise, a promise to obey what called you to this path. It is a promise to heed the awake aspect of your own mind. It is a promise to follow your spiritual aspirations, wherever they take you. It is a promise to obey the wisdom at the very core of your being.

To do so, you cannot rely solely on the rational or conceptual minds. Initially, you follow your teacher's spiritual instruction and guidance. You are navigating territory that you do not know, and your teacher fulfills one or more roles — an example of what it means to be awake, a source of transmission, an instructor in the methods of practice, and a guide who points out problems and pitfalls. As your experience and understanding grow, you touch a knowing that does not depend on reason or concept.

As that knowing takes expression in how you live, the full force of your promise starts to take hold: to live your commitment to awakening in every aspect of life. Here you enter the realm of samaya, the ethics of Vajrayana.

The essence of Vajrayana ethics is not to fall into reactivity and confusion. Whenever you do, you lose your connection with the clear empty knowing that is your teacher, your personal deity, and your protector. Patrul Rinpoche, the 19th century Nyingma master, wrote that maintaining samaya is like trying to keep a mirror clean in a dust storm. No matter what you do, dust keeps settling on it! Think of samaya as your connection with being awake. You may keep losing it, but you keep coming back to it.

Clear empty knowing is the heart of Vajrayana. To practice Vajrayana this knowing must mean more to you than anything the conventional world can offer. That is the essence of samaya and the essence of this promise.

CHAPTER 4

Birth: Becoming the Deity

After my first three-year retreat, I visited my aunt in England. I needed medical attention, and she was a doctor. One evening she invited a child psychiatrist and his wife for dinner. The conversation flowed smoothly until the psychiatrist asked, "What did you study in your retreat?"

I thought for a few minutes, and then replied, "We studied how to die."

"That's a conversation stopper," said his wife. An uncomfortable silence ensued.

Possibly not the best response, yet how to meet death in all its multitudinous forms constituted the vast majority of the practice curriculum in the three-year retreat. Even the unvarying routine forced me to face the fact that everything we experience comes and goes. No matter how much an incident, a feeling, or a memory consumed my attention, it very rarely had anything to do with the daily routine. There was nothing to do but let it go and if I didn't, sooner or later it would evaporate on its own — two kinds of dying.

Meditation on death and impermanence led me to understand that everything I experience is transitory, but such understanding was largely conceptual. It didn't go deep. The understanding that came through deity practice was deeper. Before I even took birth as a deity, I had to die, albeit symbolically. Then I took birth as the deity, lived a life as the deity, and then died as the deity. In each practice session, everything I was, everything I felt, and everything I thought I knew dissolved into nothing, and I took birth as the deity. At the end of each session, I died as the deity, and everything I am, everything I feel, and everything I know arose again—out of nothing. Day after day, month after month, year after year, I engaged that cycle. It changed how I saw life. I saw through, at least in part, the enchantments all of us live under—the illusory reality of sensory experience, of emotions, of transcendent experiences, and of control.

Deity practice is usually presented in two phases, creation and completion. Roughly speaking, creation phase is about being born and completion phase is about dying. There is a bit more to them than that, but birth and death are good places to start. This and the next two chapters cover these elements of the practice.

Birth: Creation Phase

After the empowerment ritual, your teacher gives you the oral authorization for the practice text of your deity and a copy of the practice text itself. Practice texts vary in complexity. The most elaborate give detailed descriptions of the deity's world, the deity's palace and its architectural features, and how they all come into being. They describe the deity's form, each of the faces (of multi-headed deities), what each hand holds, what the deity wears, and how all the attendant deities are positioned with respect to the main deity, their colors, what they wear, and what they hold in their hands, and so on. At the other extreme are very short practice texts that touch on only the main points.

Think of a practice text as a piece of sheet music. The sheet has notes, but the notes are not the music. The music is what happens when you play the notes. What you experience depends on how you play the notes. Do you play in tune? Do you make mistakes? Do you play at the right tempo? Do you play the music with expression? Do you give life to the music, or does it come out sounding a bit mechanical?

Through practice, you learn to play the notes correctly. You learn to play them in tune and in tempo. You learn when to play louder and when to play softer. You gradually learn from your mistakes and you begin to inject real feeling into the music. From time to time, the music becomes magical. It seems to play itself. It flows, it swells, it expresses sadness, joy, anger, or peace. You may even forget everything else and become one with the music.

This is what creation phase is like. The practice text sets out the sequence to follow to create the experience of being the deity. Through practice, you bring the deity to life and you learn how to experience yourself and your life as the deity.

To this end, you reverse the way you regard life. In each practice session, you live a life as the deity. In the periods between practice sessions your ordinary life is seen as the *bardo,* a strange, bewildering intermediate state between death as the deity at the end of a practice session and rebirth as the deity in your next practice session. The daily happenings of regular life — the struggles, the joys, the tribulations — you regard as dreams, phantoms, or hallucinations. You navigate these ups and downs as best you can, but every time you sit down to practice, you do so with the view that your time in the bardo of conventional life has come to an end, and you are taking birth again as who you truly are — White Tara.

As with the Niguma practice, in this and the following chapter I guide you through a practice text for White Tara. The name of the text is *Mastery of the Deathless.* It was written by Jamgön Kongtrul sometime in the 19th century. Again, the complete text is in the appendices.

FROM THE PRACTICE TEXT:

Refuge and awakening mind

> I take refuge in my teacher, union of the Three Jewels.
> In order to help others, I practice being the goddess
>   Wishing Wheel.

Repeat three times.

Generation of goodness (optional)

I am Tara. Light shines from my heart
And invites her and her heirs to appear before me.

vajra samaja

I go for refuge to the Three Jewels.
I acknowledge each and every unwholesome act.
I rejoice in the virtue of all beings.
I hold to the awakening of buddhas.
Until I awaken I take refuge
In the Buddha, the Dharma, and the Noble Assembly.
In order to take full care of others and myself
I form the mind of awakening.
In forming this intention for true awakening
I welcome all beings as my guests.
By immersing myself in the joyful activity of awakening,
May I awaken fully and help all beings.

Repeat this prayer, let the gathering dissolve, and then rest without reference.

May all beings be happy, be free from struggle,
Never want for joy, and rest in great equanimity.

INSTRUCTION:

First, recall your teachers and the lineages of practice that come through them. Reach out to them, praying to them to lift you out of your struggles, out of your emotional reactivity, and out of your confusion. Through their inspiration and energy you reconnect with who and what you are, the timeless awareness that is White Tara. Soon you will take birth as her.

Sit quietly for few minutes and let body and mind settle. Let your breath settle, too. Take a few long gentle breaths and then let your breathing come naturally. Ask yourself, "What am I doing?" and let the question sink in. Let it sink in until you feel something deep in your heart and body, until you touch an unfathomable peace, a clarity of mind and heart, and unlimited possibilities. That is what you are doing—orienting your being to peace, clarity, and possibilities.

That, in essence, is refuge in the Three Jewels. The peace is Buddha, the clarity Dharma, and the unlimited possibilities the Sangha, the Noble Assembly.

Then ask yourself, "Why am I doing this?" and go through the same process, letting the question sink in until you touch the groundlessness of experience and the pain of the world. A wish, an intention, and a path arise on their own. You wish for others to be free, you will do whatever it takes to help them, and you undertake this practice for those reasons.

This, in essence, is awakening mind. The groundlessness brings out the wisdom aspect of awakening mind, the pain of the world brings out the compassion aspect.

Then touch what it is like to be White Tara and let mind and body relax. A beacon of light shines from your heart inviting White Tara and all buddhas and bodhisattvas, wherever they may be in time and space. They gather in the sky in front of you, throngs upon throngs, graceful, joyful, and radiant. You join your hands in prayer and pray to them, again taking refuge, confessing all the ill and harm you have caused others because of the confusion and reactivity that troubles you in your conventional life, and rejoicing in the good that others do. You continue to pray, recalling the mind of all buddhas, the groundlessness of experience, and again engendering both the intention to help others be free of the struggles of samsaric experience and the joyful engagement of the practices and ways of living that bring that end about.

Then let everything go. Sit quietly and at ease, your heart filled with loving kindness, compassion, joy, and equanimity for all beings everywhere, as you wait to die and be born as White Tara.

Creation Phase: Birth

FROM THE PRACTICE TEXT:

om shunyata jñana vajra svabhava atma koñ ham

INSTRUCTION:

I am empty timeless awareness.

Say these words. What happens? Even if you have only a vague idea what these words mean, something usually happens. For a moment, thinking stops. The mind that you ordinarily rely on in your life, the thinking mind, just stops. Maybe it stops for only a moment, but that is enough. These words are a spell, a spell that breaks the enchantment of the conceptual mind. When you say these words, you step out of your life as you ordinarily know it, and that is a kind of death.

Say these words again, "I am empty timeless awareness." When your mind stops, who are you? Don't answer. Just rest right there. You fall into distraction soon enough. Thinking starts and attention dissipates. However, as you grow more familiar with this shift, you are able to rest in it. You notice that there is nothing there — absolutely nothing. That is emptiness.

This emptiness is not just a blankness. There is another quality, a clarity, an ineffable, indescribable clarity. Rest in the emptiness and clarity together.

In that emptiness and clarity, there is also a knowing, a way of experiencing that is just there. It isn't conceptual and it cannot be described. That way of experiencing, that way of knowing, is everything. It is what becomes the deity and it is what becomes the deity's world.

When you practice these shifts, you may try to think your way through them, but thinking does not work. In all aspects of deity practice, when you notice you are thinking, stop. Take a breath if you need to, but stop. Then drop into clear empty knowing, or empty clear experiencing (they are not different), and continue.

◇◇◇

When you practice by thinking these shifts are taking place or by imagining you are the deity, or visualizing yourself as the deity, or thinking you are the deity, you are thinking your way through this practice instead of being the deity. Twenty years later, if you are still doing deity practice, you wonder why nothing has changed. Nothing changed because you never left the conceptual mind.

A woman came to me to learn meditation. When I asked why, she replied that she wanted to experience her life. "In my generation," she said, "as far back as I can remember, I have experienced my life through a screen. First it was a television screen, then a computer screen. Now it's a mobile screen, or a tablet screen, but it's still a screen. Everything takes place through a screen. I want to experience life directly."

The conceptual mind is also a screen. It filters, shapes, and distorts experience and presents its representation as what is real. The image of a tree or a car on a computer screen is not a tree or a car. It is an image. In the same way, your concept of tree or car is not a tree or a car. The conceptual mind presents a representation of life. To know life itself, you need to go through and beyond the representation. The conceptual mind cannot do this. Thus, in deity practice, it is essential to keep coming back to the non-conceptual mind and letting the drama of the deity and the deity's world unfold there.

To engage deity practice effectively, stay in the clear empty knowing that is just there when you recite the spell. Rest right there and let the practice unfold. In what follows, you may say that it is impossible to do these practices without thinking. At first it does not seem possible, but through practice, you may discover a way.

From the sound of *hūm*, the energy of emptiness,
A protective enclosure of vajras appears.
Inside arises a palace of crystal
With a full moon throne on a white lotus flower.
The syllable *tam* appears and becomes
A white lotus flower bearing a *tam*.
Light shines from the flower and fulfills the two aims.
The light returns and the flower transforms:
Now I am Tara, white as the moon.
My smile is charming and peaceful.
Lights of five colors shine from my body.
My forehead, face, hands, and feet are graced by
The seven eyes of timeless awareness.
My right hand gestures in peerless giving;
My left holds with ring finger and thumb
A white lotus flower close to my heart.
I wear a white blouse, a five-colored skirt,
And elegant jewelry set with pearls and stones.
My black hair is bound up with locks hanging freely.
I sit in vajra posture with a moon at my back.

INSTRUCTION:

Touch that knowing, the empty clear knowing of your own mind.
It reverberates with a sound beyond the dimensions of human consciousness. The sound takes form as a huge dome, vast beyond imagination. The floor of the dome is a single vajra cross, thousands of
kilometers from tip to tip. Smaller vajra crosses fill the gaps, and still
smaller crosses fill the smaller gaps, and so on—a self-replicating
pattern that covers the whole floor. A wall of vajras standing verti-
cally forms the perimeter, with smaller and smaller vajras filling all
the interstices. The vajras arch up to form a canopy high, high above.

It, too, is made of vajras in vajras in vajras. Outside, the fires of timeless awareness blaze with the intensity of the fires at the end of time, incinerating anything and everything that touches them. The vajra floor, the vajra walls, the vajra dome all form a circle of protection, an invincible barrier to the chaos outside, the chaos and confusion inherent in conceptual knowing. You are the protection circle. The protection circle is you.

Where does this protection circle come from? It does not come from anywhere. It is this clear empty knowing. You are not imagining the dome. You are its immense vastness, its protective shielding, and the utter peace and freedom it affords. Don't imagine or visualize these qualities. Rest in clear empty experience and let those qualities arise. As they seep into you, let them take form as the protection circle.

In the center, right at the juncture of the vajra cross, a crystal palace of awakening mind arises. Its columns, beams, walls, banners, and other decorations represent the thirty-seven factors of awakening. You are this palace. This palace is you.

Again, clear empty knowing reverberates, this time with the sound of Tara's seed syllable, the syllable *tam*. The sound takes form as *tam*, the written form of the syllable, white, the same color as White Tara. Again, don't visualize this, don't imagine this. You are the sound, you are the syllable.

You now become a white lotus—the symbol of White Tara. As the symbol, you radiate light to the farthest corners of the universe. It touches the buddhas of the ten directions and three times and returns with their energy and blessing. Again you radiate light to the far corners of the universe. This time it touches each and every sentient being in samsara, instantly relieving them of all struggles and awakening them to the empty clear knowing that they are. Light shines from them and you draw it into you. Now you take birth as White Tara, your body vivid, clear, and empty, like a rainbow or a hologram, white in color, arrayed in silks and jewelry, the right hand extended in the gesture of generosity, the left holding a white lotus.

◇◇◇

Like the protection circle, everything here—the palace, the world, your body, you as White Tara—is clear empty knowing. You may think it strange that this mythic world is your mind, but this is precisely how it is in a dream. A world appears, you move in it and you interact with it, but everything—the dreamworld, the people in it, you, and what you do there—is you. It is your mind. It is what you experience. It is what you know. People often say it is in your mind, but it is more accurate to say that it is your mind. Whether through your efforts in practice, through the blessing of your teacher or the lineage, or through the protectors watching over you in your life, when mystical knowing arises, self and other drop away and you experience everything that arises as mind. You know that what you experience is empty, that it is not real in the ordinary sense of that word, that it is not separate from you, and that there is nothing actually there. Yet you experience it all the same, sometimes more vividly and more clearly than in ordinary life.

Being the Deity

Creation phase is often described in terms of a three-fold purity: pure clarity, pure recollection, and divine pride. Classically, pure clarity is the clear appearance of the form of the deity, pure recollection is knowing the symbolic meanings in the deity's form, and divine pride is the experience of being the deity.

Pure clarity

In 1974 I was translating for Dezhung Rinpoche. A student asked about visualization practice and deity meditation. Dezhung Rinpoche closed his eyes and scrunched his forehead. He bobbed his head up and down as if he were concentrating very hard and said, "You visualize the head of the deity, then you visualize all the arms, then you visualize the implements, then the palace, then you try to see the whole deity clearly, but you lose one part. You go back to visualize that... and it's all gone. You start again, and the same thing happens. Again and again!" He opened his eyes, leaned forward and laughed, "And then you have a headache!"

Do deity practice from the clear empty mind. You will avoid headaches and a lot of other problems, too. To uncover the ability to know without thinking, try this exercise. Pick up a stone and look at it. What does it mean to know the stone? If you think, "This is a stone," you are immediately separated both from the stone and from knowing the stone. Hold the stone and let any ideas about what it is move through your mind like ripples on a pond or clouds in the sky. After a while, you may find that there is no you and no stone, but an immediacy of experience in which you do not feel separate from the stone. Right there, you are beginning to know the stone.

Familiarize yourself with the deity's form and world. Traditional instructions are to look at a picture of the deity. Rest attention on a picture and take in every detail. Don't think about being the deity. Just rest attention on the deity's form and come back to it when thoughts distract you. Whether you do this in formal sessions or during the day makes no difference. The point is to plant the deity's form and attributes firmly in your mind. How you do so depends on latent talent, finding a way of working that works for you, and the amount of time you practice. In this respect, the development of the basic skills in deity meditation are similar to the development of basic skills in any other discipline.

When you are thoroughly familiar with the form of the deity and all his or her attributes, start cultivating the sequence described in the practice text in clear empty knowing. To paraphrase The Heart Sutra, White Tara is clear empty knowing, clear empty knowing is White Tara.

As long as you are touching that clear empty knowing, thoughts come and go on their own. As soon as you engage them, the clear empty knowing is gone and you are lost in thought. Whenever you are distracted, return to that clear empty knowing. In clear empty knowing, everything is there, but without the same sense of solidity. It's a bit like you are dreaming. If you stay there a little longer, you may notice that the sense of otherness is not as pronounced. The moment you start thinking about what you experience, however, the sense of otherness and subject-object duality return. When that happens, touch that clear empty knowing again and rest there.

To become White Tara, first touch that clear empty knowing. At that moment, you are her. Don't visualize. Don't imagine. Be White Tara. Let her form and her world arise on their own, from your intention and nothing else. The more deeply you rest in clear empty knowing, the more clearly and vividly you experience being the deity. The moment you start to visualize, the moment you start thinking, the moment you try to make something happen, you fall back into the conceptual mind. The spirit of White Tara evaporates and the magic disappears.

At first, her form and her world may not arise at all. It doesn't matter. Keep resting in clear empty knowing — that is the deity. Slowly, over time, White Tara's spirit takes hold in you and her form and world arise more clearly. That is how you practice pure clarity.

Pure recollection

One summer I visited Yosemite National Park. I hiked up the trail to Vernal Falls. It's a steep rocky trail, and the river tumbles over boulders that have fallen this way and that in the gorge. As the water cascades from rock to rock, it throws up clouds of spray. A fine mist hangs in the air. That morning, everywhere I looked rainbows greeted my gaze. I climbed through one rainbow after another, the colors of the spectrum as vivid as can be, but nothing solid anywhere.

When you stay in that clear empty knowing and let White Tara and the White Tara's world arise like a rainbow, everything changes — how you experience your body, your sensory faculties, and what appears to you through your senses. This is a fundamentally different way of experiencing life. It does not involve the conceptual mind. There is no self or other. There is no perceiver or perceived. Practice consists of resting in the experience of empty appearance, with your body and everything around you arising like a rainbow—clear, vivid, and empty of solidity.

The traditional instruction for pure recollection is to recall the symbolic meaning of each aspect of the deity's form. White Tara's white form, for instance, represents the purity of emptiness, her smiling expression represents compassion, the three eyes in her face see the past, present, and future, the eyes in the palms of her hands and the soles of her feet are the union of compassion and emptiness, and so on. You recall these symbolic meanings to undermine the tendency to use the deity as a new version of you. However almost all the teachers with whom I studied said that recalling the meaning of every aspect of the deity's form involved too much thinking. Instead, they said, practice pure recollection by being the deity and letting the deity's body and world appear clearly and be empty at the same time, like a rainbow.

Every deity has a personality, qualities that they express through their being. White Tara expresses an extraordinary peace, a limitless generosity, and a vibrant well-being. Other deities express their qualities in multiple heads, arms, or legs. The four arms of Great Compassion, for instance, express the four immeasurables. When you rest in the experience of being your personal god, your being absorbs the qualities of your deity. How you see and experience the world changes, right down to the level of how you know where you are, how your ordinary body is, and how it moves. You do not do the reconfiguring. It is not something you make happen through the imagination or the conceptual mind. It happens on its own, when you let the conceptual structure of who you are drop away. To live in clear empty knowing is a fundamentally different way of knowing and experiencing life. It takes time and practice to adjust to it.

Divine pride

Rest in clear empty knowing, let White Tara's form be present, and be White Tara. Do not think that you are White Tara. Be White Tara. Again, an exercise may help.

Say to yourself, "I visualize myself as White Tara." What happens? When I do this, even if I can generate a clear image of White Tara, the image feels artificial. I don't feel much connection with it. Now say to yourself, "I imagine I am White Tara." Again, what happens? When I do this, I feel more like I am White Tara, but there is still a sense of separation and a strange contradiction — I am imagining that I am something else. Set both of those approaches aside. Say, "I am White Tara." What happens then? For me, at least, there is a shift in which the thoughts, ideas, beliefs, and assumptions that ordinarily support my sense of self drop away.

Divine pride is pure pride. It is the experience of being a god empty of self. It is a knowing in which your ordinary sense of self is a movement in mind, just like any other thought, feeling, or belief. You cannot eliminate your sense of self by an act of will. It is absurd to say, "I am going to eliminate my sense of self!" By resting deeply in clear empty knowing and letting the spirit of the deity take over in you, however, you can experience being someone else. You, as you ordinarily conceive of yourself, are no longer there. A shift takes place and you know through your own experience that your sense of self is not fixed and that the world you experience is not something separate from you. That shift is the essence of divine pride, of being the deity.

When you add in the form of the deity — in White Tara's case, a white body, a gently smiling face, seven eyes, silk robes, exquisite jewelry, etc. — the shift becomes a leap. Not everyone is able to make it. Not everyone resonates with this approach. This is the difference between the sutra path and the mantra path. In the sutra path you start with the genesis of awakening, buddha nature, and build the abilities and capacities that enable you to recognize mind nature. In the mantra path, or Vajrayana, you step into the result—the deity, clear empty knowing—and let your whole being attune to being awake.

Empty Experience

The aim of deity practice is to experience what you are in a different way, a way free from the projections of thought and feeling. This way of experiencing is empty experience, though it is also translated as pure experience, pure appearance, or pure vision.

Shifts into empty experience are not brought about by an act of will. They happen as if by accident, but they are usually the result of circumstances, conditions, and training. In the case of deity practice, the level of energy in your attention is raised through dropping into empty clear knowing, through experiencing the deity and the deity's world arising, through ritual and prayer, and through other practices. That higher level of energy makes shifts into empty experience possible.

One day in my second three-year retreat, I washed a dish in the kitchen and dried my hands on a dish towel. This so angered another retreatant that he chased after me, spun me around, punched me in the face, and knocked me to the ground. As I fell, I exploded, not in pain or anger, but in a brilliant clarity, as if a sun was blazing inside my head. I was not hurt, and as I stood up, I did not feel a trace of anger. I just marveled at the extraordinary brilliance of everything—the rich vibrant green of the trees, the brilliant white of the plaster walls of the retreat cells, the peace and serenity of the cloister. I began to say something to my assailant, some words of gratitude I think, but he took one look at me and ran to his room.

Whenever you touch that clear empty knowing, you undermine the operation of the conceptual mind. If you do not touch that clear empty knowing in deity practice, you can practice for eons, and nothing will change. The deity is clear empty knowing, the deity's form is clear empty knowing, the deity's world is clear empty knowing, and you are clear empty knowing. The essential commitment in Vajrayana is to come back to that clear empty knowing again and again, in the same way that a practitioner of basic meditation comes back to resting attention in the experience of breathing.

You have just taken birth as White Tara. Take some time now and become familiar with being White Tara. Don't start mantra recitation right away. Just practice being White Tara. In particular, listen to the different parts of you and how they react or respond to your being White Tara. Some parts of you may not like being White Tara. Some may rebel. You are White Tara. What do you do with those parts that rebel? You can't dismiss them. You can't ignore them. You can't indulge them. What do you do? Most of the time, the best way to practice is to do nothing with those parts: don't ignore, don't indulge, don't block. Just be White Tara and let them work out their own relationship with this different way of being.

Be White Tara. Rest in knowing you are White Tara. Be White Tara and be in her world. Sometimes your sense of being White Tara will be clear and vivid, and sometimes not so clear. Treat such fluctuations like the weather. Sometimes the sky is clear and sometimes it is not so clear, but clear or not clear, it is still the sky.

Jamgön Kongtrul, the great 19th century master, put it this way:

When the deity's form is clear, the clear knowing is your mind.
When you're unhappy because it is not clear, that is still
        your mind.
When you want it to be clear, what keeps trying is your mind.
Timeless awareness, guru, and deity are also your mind.
Everything you experience is your mind, yet mind nature
        does not change —
Ultimately, this is the most important point of creation
        and completion.
No matter where you are in creation phase practice,

If you make awareness clear and just keep it from wandering,
Clarity arises as clear and empty and haziness as hazy
and empty.

As long as you touch clear empty knowing and let the deity's form be there, like a dream or a mirage, however clear or hazy you may be, you are practicing creation phase.

CHAPTER 5

Life: Living as the Deity

What do you do with your life?

A timeless question, but now that you are White Tara, its time has come with added poignancy. Conventional answers—happiness, wealth, fame, respect—are almost laughable in their irrelevance. You have to dig deeper. As White Tara, what do you do with your life?

Union with the Primordial White Tara

FROM THE PRACTICE TEXT:

> My three points are marked by *om, ah, and hūm.*
> Light from them invites the awareness-being: *vajra samaja.*
> *ja hūm bam ho:* she and I are one.

INSTRUCTION:

You are White Tara. You sit in a crystal palace on a lotus and moon throne. Delicate elegant silks drape your white body. Gold jewelry set with diamonds, sapphires, emeralds, rubies, and topaz highlights your every feature. You have seven eyes. The eye in your forehead looks into the essence of being. The two other eyes that grace your countenance take in the infinities upon infinities of beings that arise, abide, and vanish in the countless world systems that themselves come and go over eons in the vastness of infinite space. Four more eyes, on the palms of your hands and the soles of your feet, take in the pain and confusion of every being in every world. With a combination of understanding and compassion you see how each and every one of them struggles in their lives. Your ability and willingness

87

to help them are expressed in your right hand, extended in a gesture of unending giving. Your left holds at your heart the stem of a lotus flower that blooms by your head, a reflection of the utter purity that is present even in the swamp of samsara. You sit relaxed and at ease, the consummate serenity in your bearing devoid of any trace of self-consciousness or self-importance.

From your forehead, throat, and heart (body, speech, and mind) send light out to buddhas and bodhisattvas in every realm of every universe, calling on them to invest you with their awareness and energy. Touch their power, understanding, and compassion — its incomprehensible depth and scope coming from a level of being that transcends time and space. Summon that awareness and energy with the words, "Vajra, come here."

Millions and millions of White Taras, some as big as mountains, others as small as snowflakes, rain out of the sky and dissolve into you. Your whole being vibrates like a great bell. You are now White Tara in a different way: White Tara, master of all you behold; White Tara, timeless and ever present; White Tara, groundless experience; White Tara, empty, clear, immediate awareness, undisturbed by any thought of existence or non-existence, being or not being, self or other; White Tara, the energy and awareness of all buddhas in the three times and the ten directions.

Touch now the purpose of your life, the sole reason why you are here: to help beings know in themselves a peace that is inexpressible in words, a peace that transcends understanding, a peace that immediately frees all who touch it from the confusion and reactivity of samsara.

◇◇◇

In this section you give form to a shift that takes place naturally as practice deepens. In the birth section, you became White Tara, letting the experience of being her arise in the clear empty knowing that is mind nature. This Tara is called the connection-being, your connection with being White Tara. As you experience being White Tara, clear, empty of solidity, and empty of self, you draw in a higher level of energy, the energy of the primordial White Tara—the White Tara who is the awareness and compassion of buddha, of awake-mind. This primordial Tara is called the awareness-being. Timeless awareness joins with spiritual connection. You become White Tara as she has always been.

What is the connection between this ritual element and your life? Let's say you train to be a doctor or a mechanic. As you accumulate understanding and experience, you become what a doctor or a mechanic has always been, a capable healer or a skillful maintainer of machines. In the process, an identity forms from your profession or career. One of the functions of this practice element is to purify your life of this identification with your career.

White Tara changes all that. When you experience even a few moments of lucid dreaming—being aware that you are dreaming while you are dreaming—you experience directly being a world you know to be your mind. That experience changes how you experience the world in which you ordinarily live. In the same way, when the primordial White Tara joins with you, you know directly what you are and what you are capable of. Thoughts, thinking, emotional reactions, and identification as this or that no longer confuse you. You know you are none of those.

There are layers of deeper magic at work here, too. When I first learned these practices, I understood them mainly in terms of my rational Western upbringing. A deity such as White Tara was a symbol, an archetype, a way of representing awake-mind for the purposes of practice. As I gained more experience, I came to appreciate that these so-called symbols embodied some kind of power. They worked at a level that I could feel but could not put into words. That appreciation led me to relate to deities more as energies or even entities. They have a power and influence that was limited neither by time or space, nor by culture or belief. Increasingly, I felt that I was tapping into something much older than Tibetan Buddhism, or older even than Indian Buddhism. Not only do these deities have a power of their own, they have a life of their own.

Where do magic and sorcery end and spiritual practice begin? It is hard to say, partly because in both Indian and Tibetan culture, the methods and practices entail both spiritual and worldly aims. Thousands of years of knowledge, experience, and expertise are present in the rituals practiced in the Tibetan tradition. From ancient times sorcerers and magicians used the four syllables *ja hūm bam ho* and the mudras (hand gestures) associated with them to catch, draw in, bind, and unite with the spirit of the deity they were propitiating. They not only knew how to summon these powers, they also knew how to let themselves be taken over by them, and how to deploy those powers for whatever purposes they chose: ideally for protection, well-being, understanding, and balance, but not infrequently for changing situations (e.g., rainmaking), attracting wealth, or affecting others beneficially or adversely.

Empowerment

FROM THE PRACTICE TEXT:

> Again I send out light and invite the buddhas of the five
>   families:
> "Empowering Deities, bestow empowerment on me."
> To this request, the deities respond:
> *om sarva tathagata ahbhishekata samaya shriye hūm.*
> With these words they confer empowerment.
> My body is filled with elixir and all impurities washed away.
> The head of the family, Amitabha, crowns me.

INSTRUCTION:

You are White Tara. Now call on the buddhas of the five families to invest you with their power and capabilities. Send out streams of light to invite them. The heads of the five families come, along with the five female buddhas, the six male bodhisattvas, the six female bodhisattvas, and the ten sentinels. Feel their presence as they gather in front of you.

The five buddhas — blue, yellow, red, green, and white — formally pronounce the words of investiture, "One by one we confer our powers on you." Their female counterparts stand over you and, from the jeweled vases they carry, pour the elixirs of the different aspects of timeless awareness into you. In celebration, the male bodhisattvas fill the air with joyous songs while the female bodhisattvas shower you with offerings — beautiful flowers and jewels, majestic music, wonderful perfumes and fragrances, delicious fruits and delicacies, exquisite silks and linens, and inspiring poetry and teachings. The ten wrathful sentinels, who have taken their positions in each of the ten directions, stamp and stomp as they brandish their weapons, warding off disturbances to this empowerment.

The elixirs of awareness course through your body, wash away all impurities, and fill your being with crystal clear light, investing you with the powers and capabilities of all buddhas throughout time and space. The overflow of the elixirs forms a tiny Buddha of Boundless Light (Amitabha) who sits on your head, your guiding principle and teacher.

Then all the empowerment deities dissolve into light, and that light pours into you.

◇◇◇

Traditional teachings on deity practice describe this empowerment ritual as purifying the stage of life in which you come into your birthright. Think of it as emptying out the sense of self, the sense of being special, that arises on those occasions when you are appointed to a position of responsibility. You are invested with power and authority, but that investiture comes with responsibilities. Those responsibilities are represented by Buddha of Boundless Light, the head of the lotus family, the buddha family that epitomizes compassion. In other words, as White Tara you now shoulder the responsibilities of awakened compassion.

Offerings and Praise

FROM THE PRACTICE TEXT:

> I send out deities who honor and praise me.
> *om arya tara vajra argham padyam pukpé dhupé aloké gendhé*
>   *névidya shapda praticha ah hūm svaha*
> (To noble Tara we offer drinking water, washing water,
>   flowers, incense, light, perfume, food, and music.)
> We gods and titans pay homage
> By laying our crowns at your feet.
> You, who save us from all catastrophes,
> Mother Savior, we honor and praise you.

INSTRUCTION:

You have come into the fullness of your power. Offering gods and goddesses pour out of your heart. They celebrate you as a royal lady returning to her palace from a long journey. They welcome you to your home, giving you refreshing spring water to drink, washing your feet with warm water, draping you with garlands of colorful flowers, lighting incense whose fragrance soothes and relaxes you, bringing candles and oil lamps whose light brings comfort and pleasure to your eyes, spraying you lightly with perfumed water, setting before you a feast that delights the eye and excites the palate, and playing music of such beauty it brings tears to your eyes.

A chorus of gods and goddesses then raise their voices, singing songs of praise, extolling all the magnificent qualities and powers that you, White Tara, can draw on to calm the struggles of beings, to enhance their health, abilities, and lives, to protect them against threats to their well-being, and to cut through problems and difficulties that stand in their way to freedom. The buddhas and bodhisattvas in the ten directions and three times look to you to continue their work. Teachers and mystics throughout the world rejoice in your intention to help all who suffer. All beings, everywhere, express their wonder and awe at your power, vitality, understanding, and compassion and rejoice that their savior has indeed arrived.

Even as you are White Tara, in your palace, surrounded by gods and goddesses, keep touching the clear empty knowing in which all this arises. Receive these bountiful offerings and songs of praise as if in a dream, without a trace of self-importance or self-consciousness.

Then all these gods and goddesses, too, dissolve into light, and that light comes into you.

◇◇◇

Again, according to traditional teachings, this ritual element purifies sensual pleasures. For instance, when people praise or compliment you, what they say is not really about you. It is an expression of the joy they are feeling. The same holds when people criticize you. The criticism is an expression of their pain or difficulty. When you drop your personal investment in the experience of praise or criticism, you relate directly to what the other person is feeling, and, in doing so, hear more clearly what they are saying.

Fulfilling White Tara's Calling

INSTRUCTION:

Let your heart blaze with brilliant light, illuminating the whole universe and striking the hearts of buddhas throughout the universe. Light streams from their hearts. Draw their light and energy into you. Let their light, energy, and awareness suffuse and merge with you.

Now turn your attention to all beings and send light from your heart to them. This light instantly dispels their confusion, reactivity, struggles, illness, and pain, just as sunlight instantly dispels darkness and gloom. In their joy, their hearts also blaze with light. Draw in their light, too. Peace and joy flood you from head to toe, the peace of freedom from reactivity and the joy of freedom from confusion.

Again and again radiate and absorb light. Touch every buddha and every buddha realm with your devotion. Touch every being and every realm in samsara with your compassion. Draw in the power and energy of awakening from all buddhas and the peace and joy of freedom from all beings. Your calling is fulfilled when every being in samsara is freed.

◇◇◇

Radiation-absorption is a method of energy transformation. In radiating light to the buddhas, you connect with a higher level of awareness and energy. You draw it in and absorb it. When you radiate light to the beings in each of the six realms, you are, in effect, bringing a higher level of awareness and energy to your own emotional reactivity. When suffused by a higher level of energy, emotional reactions break up and release energy. The higher level of awareness made possible by the released energy is experienced as one or other aspect of timeless awareness. In this practice you simulate this transformation and develop higher levels of energy, and thus create the conditions in your being for that transformation to arise on its own.

As you are able to sustain attention at higher levels of energy, attention penetrates deeper into your system, stirring up deeper levels of reactivity and confusion. Emotional reactions may erupt with little or no warning. Energy surges, powered by the energy released as emotional reactions break up, may precipitate dramatic shifts, from experiences of extraordinary joy and light to bottomless darkness and depression, from brilliant clarity to utter confusion, from profound peace to intense agitation. Don't attach any significance to these ups and downs. Keep coming back to the clear empty knowing of mind nature, rest there, and maintain balance as best you can. Let these highs and lows come and go on their own. In this way, you come to see and know them for what they are: fluctuations and movements in mind.

At one point during deity practice in my first three-year retreat, I was consumed by the idea that my life was a complete failure. Every minute of every hour of every day derisive and critical thoughts erupted with volcanic intensity: "You have accomplished nothing and will never accomplish anything! You are hopeless and will never amount to anything. You have wasted your life. You are a complete failure." These eruptions had no discernible connection with deity practice. Yet day after day, these lava bombs exploded out of nowhere and set me on fire. As best I could, I kept coming back to deity practice. I would do the meditation for a few moments, and then thoughts of failure would surge up again, blotting out any sense of being the deity. I would imagine the form, catch quick glimpses of arms or a face, only to plunge into a black pit of utter and abject failure. I tried reciting the mantra, but usually managed only a few syllables before I forgot what I was doing. I knew these thoughts were ridiculous. My life was not over. I was only thirty years old! Yet they persisted. The volcano erupted continuously for about two weeks, and then it stopped as suddenly as it had started. What happened? Where did it go? There were no logical answers. This obsession with failure was a powerful wave of internal material, no doubt. It was also a way to learn that the nature of waves is to rise and fall.

Mantra Recitation

INSTRUCTION:

Rest in the clear empty knowing of mind nature. You are White Tara, white, clear, and radiant, the expression in form of the mystical compassion of all buddhas. At some point you experience a profound stability and clarity that is unaffected by either dullness or busyness. It is as if another being has come into you, bringing with her another level of attention. This is the attention-being. She takes the form of the syllable *tam* in your heart. It stands above a white wheel with eight spokes with the letters of the mantra arranged around the *tam* and above the wheel. The letters vibrate slightly and you hear the sound of White Tara's mantra, *om taré tuttaré turé svaha*, like a continual reverberation, echoes of echoes, resounding gently with no beginning or end.

Recite Tara's mantra softly with a steady relaxed rhythm, or sing it gently over and over again.

FROM THE PRACTICE TEXT:

> In my heart there is a lotus, moon, and wheel.
> Above the center of the wheel is the syllable *tam*.
> Above and below are the syllables *om* and *ha*,
> The other eight syllables, one above each spoke
> Positioned clockwise, the color of the fall moon, clear and still.

Say the root mantra as the principal recitation:

om taré tuttaré turé svaha

INSTRUCTION:

When you recite your deity's mantra, you are praying to your personal god. With *om mani padme hūm*, for instance, you are calling to Avalokiteshvara. Mani Padme means Lotus Jewel, one of Avalokiteshvara's many names. You are also invoking the symbolic power of the deity's mantra. Mani Padme represents the union of the jewel of compassion with the lotus of emptiness. Tara's mantra is a three-fold play on her name, *taré, tu-taré, tu-ré*. The three-fold repetition indicates that she frees beings from three kinds of threats — physical, emotional, and spiritual. A mantra can also be an exhortation to action. With Mahakala's mantra, you are summoning Mahakala to eliminate interruptions and disturbances to spiritual practice. With Tara's mantra, you are asking her to save all beings.

When you make the mantra part of you, reciting it all the time, at a certain point it begins to run in you by itself, replacing the under-current of thoughts and instilling in you a stability of attention that is always there.

Mantra recitation is a way to rest when you are tired. Sit quietly and say the mantra softly, resting your attention on the sound of your voice. The recitation helps you to avoid falling into distraction. Thoughts come and go, of course, but whenever you are distracted, you return to resting in the sound. Mantra can also be a stimulus to attention, a way to stay awake and alert during practice sessions.

◇◇◇

A mantra is a spell. You are casting a spell and invoking its magic to change how the world, or something in the world, appears to you. In deity meditation, you invoke the power of the deity's secret name to transform the way you experience yourself and the world in which you live. The power of the spell comes from the emotional energy of your faith and devotion.

Mantra recitation is also a purification practice. It changes your relationship with speech and sound. Mantra becomes pure sound, and, from there, it leads to the union of sound and emptiness.

When you practice mantra recitation, it may stir up old emotional reactions. If those reactions do not release on their own, you may experience energy imbalances, including demonic possession or mental or physical illness. Disturbing dreams are often an early indicator. These imbalances take many forms — pressure in the upper torso or in the head, pressure around the heart, gastrointestinal disorders, depression, hallucinations, or strange and unpredictable behaviors, etc.

Toward the end of the second year of the three-year retreat, the year devoted to deity practice, gastrointestinal disorders started to cause me more than a little discomfort. When I asked my teacher if I could ease off the mantra recitation, his response was, "Mantra is the wind that fans the fire of samadhi."

The fire of samadhi? I couldn't find even a few glowing embers. The disorders eventually forced me to stop reciting mantras. Instead, I spent a lot more time resting. Even the slightest effort at deity practice re-excited the problems. I had to learn to rest in a way that I never had before. Taking and sending (tonglen) from Mahayana Mind-Training was the only practice I could do that did not make the problems worse. I let my system find balance as best it could, and stopped trying to make anything happen in my meditation. Difficult as it was, in retrospect, it was a valuable learning.

In several of the early practice texts I had read that mantra recitation was mainly for restoring balance, "When you are tired, relax and recite the mantra." Later, in a conversation with Thrangu Rinpoche, I learned that practitioners in Tibet were generally instructed to say mantras whenever they were practicing, whatever they were doing. "Otherwise," he said, "they just fell asleep."

Most people find mantra recitation helpful. It is a way to generate energy, a way to keep attention stable and avoid distraction, and a way to avoid falling asleep. That was not the case for me. Instead, I made a point of doing deity practice from the clear empty knowing of mind nature, letting the form of the deity arise on its own, and spending much more time with the first three elements — union with the primordial deity, the empowerment ritual, and the subsequent offerings and praise. As my system recovered its balance, I could also return to radiation-absorption practice. Even so, I took care to ease off whenever I felt out of balance or any of the symptoms of energy imbalances arose. Little by little, the energy and deep magic in these elements built in me a more balanced practice.

Later, when I taught deity practice to students, I encouraged them to spend time resting in being the deity, letting the form of the deity arise in clear empty knowing, like a cloud forming in the sky, and letting mantra recitation develop naturally, in a balanced way. That being said, individual experience varies greatly. Some people have no problem with mantra recitation and find that it brings power and energy to their practice. Other people do have problems and need to work with mantra more carefully or rely on other aspects of deity practice.

Generally speaking, if you try to direct or control the course of your spiritual development, reactive patterns in you inevitably take over. Higher levels of energy without a corresponding level of awareness amplify reactivity. When you control your experience, you ignore or repress much of what arises as well as the emotions that motivate your need to control — pride, competitiveness, unworthiness, ambition, etc. Whatever you block, however, continues to be amplified by your efforts in practice. Sooner or later, you encounter serious problems. The most serious is that you end up being torn in two — a capable practitioner and even a good teacher on the one hand, a power-hungry predator or teacher obsessed with money, sex, or control on the other. In any practice, but especially in deity and mantra practice, let the practice work on every part of you. Don't exclude or repress anything. Don't try to control what arises. Be consistent in your practice, pay attention to balance, and let the magic do its work.

Dissolution and Arising

Eons ago you took birth as White Tara. You lived a full life, developing your powers and exercising them to free beings from their struggles in samsara. Now that you have fulfilled your reason for being, your life comes to an end.

FROM THE PRACTICE TEXT:

> The world and its inhabitants melt into light.
> I, too, and the syllable *tam* melt
> Into a sheer clarity free from reference.

INSTRUCTION:

Light radiates from your heart with a brilliance brighter than the sun, illuminating not only your body, but the world around you with its palaces and grounds, the protection circle, and the cosmos beyond. Everything, even the chaos of the world outside the protection circle and every being in it, dissolves into light. That light comes into you, into your heart, into the seed syllable of the deity in your heart, and your form as White Tara dissolves into light until all that is left is the sigil *tam*. It, too, dissolves down to a tiny point of light, and then the point of light itself dissolves and disappears.

FROM THE PRACTICE TEXT:

> Again I am White Tara, marked by the three syllables.
> All experience is the play of deity, mantra, and timeless
>   awareness.

INSTRUCTION:

A distant bell, a familiar fragrance, a passing thought — something moves and you take form in your own body. Look around you. Take in the room in which you practice, the pictures on the walls, the furniture, and the floor. Listen to the sounds of life around you. Rest in the emptiness of mind and let thoughts come and go on their own. It's all there again, but not quite as before. Everything you experience is tinged with a bit of wonder, of magic, as if you are dreaming. Keep that sense of wonder and with it, the clear empty knowing in which experience arises.

Your life as White Tara has dissolved. You are still White Tara, but you are now in the intermediate state between your death as White Tara in this practice period and your rebirth as White Tara in the next.

Who are you, right now? White Tara or you? It is better not to answer this question. Instead, carry with you the feeling of being White Tara as you go about your life. Meet the challenges of the bardo, the period between death and rebirth as White Tara, without losing touch with that clear empty knowing in the flood of sights, sounds, thoughts, and feelings that make up your ordinary life.

The clear empty knowing? It is still there. It is always there. You cannot remember it but you can come back to it, and that is what you do. If you touch how it feels in your body, it is just there. Shapes and colors and objects appear as if in a dream, there and not there. Sounds, whether of a passing car or your partner cooking in the kitchen, are like echoes, there and not there. Thoughts and feelings come and go on their own, like reflections in a mirror, there and not there. As you go about your life, keep touching the mind of White Tara—a deep peace, an infinite compassion, a sense of awe and wonder, and a quiet joy in the richness of life itself.

Conclusion: Dedication, Aspiration, and Good Fortune

Through this good may I and all beings
Quickly become the mother of all buddhas, the perfection of
    wisdom.
May the noble Tara look after us in all our lives.
May the good fortune of life, energy, and timeless awareness
    fill the whole universe.

Mother of the supreme buddha Amitabha,
Reliable giver of immortality,
Blessed one, holder of knowledge,
May the good fortune of Tara prevail.

INSTRUCTION:

At the end of your practice session, sit for a few moments before you stand up and go about your day. Whether your session was difficult or easy, peaceful or chaotic, ecstatic or agonizing, you have made an effort—two efforts, actually. On the one hand, as White Tara you gave expression to a mystical level of compassion, instilling it in your being while tasting what it means to help others without prejudice, judgment, or reservation. On the other, you made an effort to step beyond your ordinary experience of life into an emptiness in which awareness and experience are not separate. These efforts may not seem like much, but they are important and they bear fruit over time.

Take a few moments now and feel in yourself the possibility of infinite compassion and unfathomable emptiness, and the peace and freedom they open. Now feel that same possibility for others. Form a wish, a wish that the good you have done will, in some strange or miraculous way, help others to make a similar effort, to know a similar peace, and to know a similar freedom. Make that wish from the bottom of your heart.

That, in essence, is dedication.

Take another few moments and form your own wishes — to understand what you yearn to understand, to experience what you yearn to experience, to know what you yearn to know. Find one or two prayers that speak to you, and say them at the end of your practice session. There are literally hundreds of such prayers, but the main point is to form those aspirations and carry them into your day. You will find one such prayer, *Niguma's Mystical Wishes*, in the postscript of this book.

That, in essence, is aspiration.

Finally, take a few moments to wish good fortune for the world and all beings in it. Good fortune is whatever brings peace, understanding, and ease to body, mind, and heart. Again, make a wish that the white flowers of good fortune rain down from the sky on every being, healing their bodies, calming their fears, and bringing understanding and peace to their minds.

This, in essence, is good fortune.

Now go about your day.

CHAPTER 6

Death: Dying as the Deity

An aspiring hermit had received the empowerment and meditation instruction for the deity Vajra Terrifier (Sanskrit: Vajrabhairava). Vajra Terrifier is a very wrathful deity with multiple heads, multiple arms, and multiple legs. Each hand holds a different weapon and each foot stands on a different god or goddess. Most notably, a pair of gigantic horns protrude from his principal head.

The hermit went into the mountains and found a suitable cave to dwell in. A small opening protected him from the elements, and a high ceiling and large interior provided a good living space. After many years he became Vajra Terrifier, but then he had a problem. With the gigantic horns he could not fit through the small opening of the cave. He was stuck in his cave.

In his enthusiasm he had taken the deity as a solid entity. It took a while, but he came to see his mistake. He then practiced for several more months until Vajra Terrifier's form arose like a rainbow, vivid and empty. Then he could come and go without problem.

Such stories are myths, or mythical in nature—timeless truths passed down in what appear to be improbable anecdotes. One way to understand this story is that it describes the relationship between creation phase and completion phase. The creation of the deity, the experience of being the deity, has to be completed with the experience of emptiness.

You have become White Tara. In her mythic realm you are able to draw on the wisdom, power, and energy of all buddhas past, present, and future. You bring untold help to untold multitudes of beings in all of the six realms. You are even able to traverse the intermediate state, the bardo between death and birth, without losing awareness.

Deep inside you, however, chthonic forces begin to stir. Long-forgotten yearnings begin to assert themselves. More and more you think, "I am White Tara. I am not subject to death. I live forever. I live in bliss, free from pain, free from struggle. I am completely pure, unburdened by the dross of existence. I am one with all I behold, and I behold everything. I..., I..., I...." Without realizing it, you have become a cosmic monster.

This is the one drawback of creation phase practice. A sense of self based on the deity can arise. It may be subtler than the ordinary sense of self, but it binds you all the same. Demonic obsessions arise, the dark forces stirred up by creation phase practice. They take energy from attention and awareness and divert it to satisfy deep yearnings — a yearning for immortality, a yearning for utter purity, a yearning for eternal bliss, or a yearning for universal selfhood.

These are old and deep obsessions, demonic in their power. They have captivated people in every age and every culture. How many religions, how many philosophies, and how many cults have promised immortality, purity, bliss, or universal selfhood in one form or another?

At the end of the previous chapter, you died as White Tara. With the completion of your life's purpose you allowed your experience of being White Tara to dissolve into light until nothing was left but the clear empty knowing called mind nature. This practice is one form of completion phase. It is called unmediated completion phase, completion phase unmediated by another practice. However, that dissolution is not always enough to dispel the enchantments of the four demonic obsessions. Some people need a higher level of energy and awareness, a level that is developed through mediated completion phase, completion phase practice mediated by energy transformation.

In general, energy is transformed when you open to what you experience and stay in that experience without reacting to it, without acting on it, without suppressing it. With a sufficiently high level of energy powering attention, you are able to stand in the presence of these four obsessions and know them for what they are — movements in mind. When you know experientially that they are nothing other than movements in mind, you are no longer caught by them and you are no longer in danger of becoming a cosmic monster. You are truly free.

One such completion phase practice is the magical apparition practice (illusory body) from the Six Teachings of Niguma. It is centered on the magical quality of life. As Niguma herself once said:

Experience arises like magic.
If you practice like magic
You awaken like magic
Through the power of faith.

Magical Apparition through Devotion

Niguma's first instruction is:

Everything compounded is impermanent. I can die at any time. What is the point of my being here? As my deity, I pray with deep devotion to my teacher who sits above my head. Then he (she) merges with me and I relax and rest, cutting through the complexities of the three times.

INSTRUCTION:

Look around you. Flowers bloom, fade, dry, and fall. Trees grow from shoot to sapling, from sapling to tree, from tree to fallen log rotting on the forest floor. Mountains crumble into sand. Rivers change their courses. Lakes dry up. Even the oceans change. Towns and cities, houses and skyscrapers, stores and factories all come and go, as do all living beings, from the smallest insect to the largest elephant.

Listen. Every sound you hear right now will stop or fade away. No sound, however melodious, however discordant, however enchanting, lasts forever. Smells, tastes, and textures are the same, here for a few moments and then gone, as if they had never been.

Everything you experience passes — everything you experience through the senses; every thought, idea, or theory; every emotion, whether anger, greed, love, or joy; even every hope and every fear. So too with every idea you have about yourself or anyone else, every belief, and every identity. Everything changes, sometimes from one moment to the next, sometimes over the course of years, decades, or even centuries. The scale may differ, but everything succumbs to the passage of time.

Look at a reflection of a flower in a mirror. What is it? The flower's reflection appears vividly, but there is no actual flower there. Sit for a few minutes, resting attention on the flower's reflection while resting in the knowing that it is not a flower. Then open to the impermanence of everything you experience and let it sink in. At the same time, rest in the clear empty knowing you know from teacher-union practice. Sit with both of these together. What happens? Everything you experience, inside and outside, takes on a dream-like quality.

Now do the same without a mirror. Look at an object — a chair, a computer, a flower, or a book, and open to the transience of sensory experience. Rest attention on the object, knowing it without thinking about it, knowing it too will pass. Do the same with other objects, and then with your other senses, hearing, taste, touch, and smell. Then look inside — look at what you think, what you believe, and what you feel. Thoughts, beliefs, and emotions also come and go. Experience them, knowing them to be transient.

When you practice this way, you experience what arises externally and internally without having to do anything with any of it. A different kind of attention forms. Distractions, distortions, and personal agendas fall away. The usual projections of thought and feeling don't arise, or, if they do, they don't take hold. This shift is one indication of energy transformation.

Practice this shift again and again throughout the day, becoming familiar with it in every situation you encounter in your life. What you see and experience may seem less solid, and you, yourself, may feel lighter, clearer, and freer. Neither your body nor your mind is used to experiencing life this way.

Make small movements to orient body, speech, and mind. For instance, touch a book or a plate before you pick it up. When you put down a glass, touch the table with it before you put it down. When you sit down, touch the seat with your hand. When you stand up, feel how your feet take the weight of your body. Take a breath before you say anything. When you do speak, listen to the sound of your own voice as if you are listening to an echo. Don't act on thoughts and feelings. Instead, without blocking thoughts and feelings, touch the space in which they arise, and let clear empty knowing inform what you do and what you say.

When you have familiarized this way of experiencing life, let the question "Am I ready to die?" arise. Don't think about it. Just pose the question. At first, a flood of memories and regrets, triumphs and failures, missed opportunities, hopes, and fears may overwhelm you. Don't block them. Don't dismiss them. Don't indulge them. Don't observe them. Rest, awake and aware in the flood, holding the question, "Am I ready to die?" Rest in the sky of non-conceptual knowing and let these thoughts and feelings form and dissolve on their own.

Time and again, you recognize that a regret, a shameful memory, a connection, or a source of joy has taken over. As soon as you recognize that, start again. Pose the question and rest, clear and awake. If you fall into observing thoughts and feelings, ask, "What observes?" and rest right there. Let this way of experiencing seep into your whole being until you are thoroughly familiar with it.

Then turn to the question, "What am I doing here?" Don't try to answer the question. Just let the question be there and rest in any shift that takes place. Different voices come out of the woodwork, voices that tell you what you should or should not be doing. Other voices, other thoughts and feelings, arise in reaction. Don't block them, don't observe them. Whenever you fall into distraction or observing, come back to a clear empty knowing and rest there. Let the thoughts, feeling, images, and voices resolve themselves. Don't observe them. Don't track them. The sky does not block, track, or observe clouds. White or black, big or small, clouds form out of nothing and dissolve into nothing. In the same way, be what knows the arising and let what arises resolve itself. Just as waves in the ocean are the movement of the ocean, thoughts, feelings, and sensations are the movement of mind. Don't think about this. Rest in clear empty knowing until you experience them this way.

These three practices — seeing the world as reflections, taking in death and impermanence, and looking at what you are doing in life — challenge the assumptions, patterns, and conditioning underneath the seeming solidity of an external world, of thoughts and feelings, and of spiritual ideals. To break the spell of solidity, take another step. Let the spirit of your deity come into you, and become him or her. Feel the presence of your teacher above you, let your heart open, and reach out. Reach out to your teacher, this person or figure who embodies what you yearn to know, and pray. The words you use are not as important as the reaching out.

The reaching out may hurt. It often does. This is the hurt of longing. It is a hurt that wants to be felt. As much as you are able to, feel the hurt without being swallowed by it or pushing it away. As you reach out while feeling the hurt, a clarity begins to dawn, the clarity of faith. Let the hurt of longing and the clarity of faith steep in you, steep to the point that all thinking subsides. Rest. Rest in pain and in faith. Rest in peace and in clarity. Your teacher dissolves into light and comes into your heart. Now rest there. At this point, another shift may arise. You step out of time — no past, no present, no future.

Magical Apparition through Intention

Niguma's second instruction:

> In every moment make three practices active: form as deity, devotion to teacher, and intention to know experience as magic.

Everything, the world around you and all that moves in it, appears but does not exist as such, like an enchantment, like a dream. Keep recognizing mind nature without fixating on anything.

INSTRUCTION:

Become your deity. By now you are able to move into being your deity without a lot of ceremony. As your deity, touch the clear empty knowing that is there whenever thinking and conceptualizing stop. From there, reach out to your teacher to bring out your faith and devotion. Pray to know experience as a magical apparition. Prayer and devotion open the possibility of the shift you seek. Pray as long and as deeply as you need to feel your faith and devotion clearly. Then add to the mix your yearning to know the magical nature of experience. How deep does that yearning go in you? Go all the way to the bottom and let that yearning become your intention. Work with these three practices — being your deity, devotion to your teacher, and holding intention — until you can be in all three at the same time. It may take you a few weeks or months before you can do so with any facility.

As you hold all three, open to everything you see, hear, taste, touch, smell, think, feel, and believe. Open to the experience of everything and everyone. When you open, you may experience a subtle shift, maybe just a glimmer at first, as if you are in a dream. Rest right there. Don't try to do anything with it — it may be just a momentary glimmer. When it passes, rest for a few minutes, and then go through the same sequence again. Keep doing this until you run out of juice. The shift probably won't happen every time, but bit by bit, you are able to rest longer in the experience that everything is mind.

When you are able to rest in that shift for short periods of time, start looking at your mind. Look at what experiences. Look at what knows. This is like looking at a mirror. You see the reflections in the mirror, but you don't see the mirror, even though you are looking right at it. Look at the reflections, but don't do anything with them.

In the same way, look at mind. You don't see mind but the looking moves you to a higher level of awareness. Don't do anything with the thoughts, feelings, and sensations that arise. They are like the reflections in the mirror. Rest in the sensory and emotional field and look. Look into the sensory and emotional field and rest. Rest in the looking. Look in the resting. Whenever attention crumbles, or when something catches you and you fall out of awareness, start again.

Don't think. Don't think your way through this practice. Thinking does not have the power or energy to change how you experience life. Whenever you recognize that you have fallen into thinking, stop. Relax for a minute or two and then start again. Become your deity. Pray to your teacher to know life as a dream. Feel your yearning and let your yearning become intention. Feel that intention in your body, in your heart, or in your abdomen. Hold deity, teacher, and intention all at the same time and then open to everything you experience. When a shift takes place, rest in the shift and look at your mind. What experiences this? What knows? Rest in the looking. Look in the resting.

◇◇◇

This is not a conceptual process. If you stay at the conceptual level, nothing changes. The combination of being the deity, feeling devotion, and holding intention raises the level of energy in your system. If you are able to drop the conceptual mind and go through these steps, sooner or later you will experience a glimmer of everything arising as a magical apparition. As you continue to practice, that glimmer becomes stronger and more stable.

Magical Apparition through Transformation

Niguma taught a third method to know and experience life as a magical apparition. The first approach relied on impermanence and devotion to precipitate a shift in how experience arises. The second approach relied on your letting go of conditioned associations (by becoming your deity), and cultivating devotion and intention. In this third approach, you pull out all the stops.

INSTRUCTION:

Drop into being your deity. Take as your deity the deity with which you have the strongest connection.

Become your deity. Your body is not solid. It is made of light, light that takes the form of your deity. It is empty inside. In your lower abdomen the womb of experience appears, an inverted triangular pyramid, a tetrahedron to be precise. It is white, open at the top, with one vertex pointing forward, the other two at each kidney, and the tip pointing straight down to the perineum. It is not solid. It, too, is made of light.

This womb of experience is the source of everything you experience. It contains the six kinds of beings. In its lowest regions are hell beings, consumed by raging fires of anger or frozen in icy wastes of hate. Above them are hungry and thirsty ghosts, starved, parched, or physically distorted by their avarice and greed. Above the ghosts are animals — domestic animals raised for food, labor, or entertainment, and wild animals leading precarious lives as prey, predator, or both. Then there are busy, busy humans, doing everything they can to satisfy their insatiable desires. Above them in turn are titans, consumed by envy and caught up in constant conflict with each other and with the gods above them. Above the titans are gods of desire, enjoying the best that life can offer until the approaching end of their lives plunges them into terror and despair. And last above them are gods of the form and formless realms, dwelling in varying degrees of stillness and tranquility until their karma dissipates and they fall into lower states of being.

Look at all these kinds of beings in the womb of experience inside you. They are there but they appear like a magical apparition, a dream, or a reflection in a mirror — there and not there. See them all clearly. See how one realm leads to another. See the potentials and propensities that shape each being's experience. There are no actual beings there — only the appearance of beings. Even though you know there are no beings there, the beings who do appear to you struggle and suffer in their lives. To them their lives are real. Enslaved by their beliefs and feelings, confined in prisons of their own making, bound by chains they themselves forged, they know no respite from their pain and difficulties. They know nothing of true peace or freedom. They cannot imagine being any other way. Even though you know these beings are your own mind, even though there are no beings there, you see all this pain and struggle, and your heart breaks. It may be all a magical apparition, but compassion for these beings still wells up inside you, caught as they are in an endless cycle of perception, reaction, struggle, and pain.

Now recall the first two lines from Niguma's poem:

Experience arises like magic.
If you practice like magic

As you feel compassion well up inside you, practice taking and sending, taking in the pain and the struggles of all these beings and giving them your peace and well-being. Do this as if you were doing it in a dream.

Take in their hatred and anger, their malice and cruelty, and their greed and blindness. Take in their struggles to make their lives better, their envy and greed, their pride and stupidity. Send out the food, clothing, and shelter you have in your own life. Send them the enjoyment you take in family and friends. Give them your talents, your skills, and your intelligence — everything you cherish in your own life. Give them the peace and joy you know deep in your heart. Touch them with the love and compassion that soothes the fires of anger and melts the ice of hate. Give them the joy that unties the knots of envy and greed. Send them the clarity that dispels the arrogance of pride and the blindness of instinct.

As you give them your own peace and well-being and take in their pain and struggles, consider what you can do to free them from their self-generated misery and pain. What can you possibly do? How can you free beings who aren't there from the struggles they themselves create in their ephemeral lives?

It is an impossible task. At your present level of understanding, you cannot imagine how it could be done. To free these beings, you have to reach out to a different way of knowing, a higher level of understanding, a deeper wisdom, and that is precisely what your teacher represents to you. Pray to your teacher. Pray, but not just for your own welfare, not just for your own peace, not just for your own freedom. Pray for the welfare, the peace, and the freedom of every being in the womb of experience and every being throughout the universe. Pray for every being who is beaten down by the tyranny of emotional reactions and imprisoned in the dungeons of conceptual experience. Pray to your teacher from the depths of your heart. Pray until your whole being is so suffused with faith and devotion that all thinking subsides.

Now turn your attention to the beings in the womb of experience inside you. Look at one being. Poof! That being disappears. Look at another. It disappears, too. Look at each of them in turn. One by one they disappear. Go through each of the six kinds of beings until the womb of experience is empty and then rest there. Let body, breath, and mind settle on their own. Rest — relaxed, at peace, and aware.

Something calls you. You and the world reappear, but now as a magical apparition, a dream, an enchantment. Go about your life, but not as before. Let a sense of wonder and magic imbue everything you see, hear, and do. Thoughts and feelings arise, but they dissolve in this sense of wonder before they take hold of you.

Inside you are quiet, deeply quiet, as if there is no one home. Yet when you speak, the right words come from your lips, though they may sound as if they come from a great distance. Any thought of transcendence has vanished from your mind. There is only what is in front of you. Whether it is pleasant or unpleasant, difficult or easy, you meet it with a sense of wonder and enchantment. You have no idea what life is, who or what you are, or what this mystery is, but you meet and embrace it — aware of details and distinctions, sensing balance and imbalance, responding to what arises, moving in a dance moment by moment.

◇◇◇

This is what it means to die as a deity. Your whole being is subsumed into mystery. The four practices at the core of all the Kagyu traditions — inner heat, magical apparition, dream, and sheer clarity — all bring you to this point, whether you experience it through the intense bliss and emptiness of inner heat, the wonder of magical apparition, the otherwordly fluidity of dream, or the sheer clarity of being itself. Your life unfolds, not in service to reactions and prejudices, but in service to the mystery of life itself.

As for the four demonic obsessions, you now know what is unchanging. Death loses its sting, and the seduction of eternal life loses its hold. Death is death, the end of life. You will meet it when your time comes. Now you know a purity that embraces both the pure and the impure. The grit and grime of life no longer threaten you, and the seduction of the pure over the impure loses its power. Life is messy, and problems arise all the time. Big or small, you address each of them in turn. You now know a happiness and joy that does not depend on illness or health. The seduction of transcendent bliss no longer beguiles you. Life is life. Your body is your body. You trust it, it breathes and sustains you, and you accept its limitations, whatever they may be. As for who or what you are, you have no idea. Nor is it a concern. You respond to what life presents to you, and you know — magically, mysteriously, yet unambiguously — that that is all there is to do.

Energy Transformation Practice

All practices in mediated completion phase are energy transformation practices. Through them you develop the levels of energy needed to meet the four demonic obsessions and other deeply conditioned patterns. But what is energy? What does it do? How do you practice it?

Energy arises from the interaction between mind and body. In Taoism it is called *chi* or *qi*, in Indian mysticism it is called *vayu*, in the Tibetan traditions it is called *rlung* (pron. lūng), in Reiki and other trainings it is called *energy*. Like mind, it is a mystery—you can experience it, but you cannot explain it. Like air or wind, it is usually experienced only when it is in motion. Like light, it spans a spectrum, operating at different levels in the mind-body system. Some traditions talk about different frequencies, extending the analogies of sound and light to explain the operation of energy at different levels. Other traditions talk about different kinds of energy, breaking them down according to how they act in the mind-body system.

The natural flow of energy gives rise to health in the body and clarity in the mind. When the natural flow of energy is disrupted by the operation of conflicting emotional reactions, for example, energy does not flow as it should. It stagnates, or may even flow the wrong way. These blockages, knots, or other constrictions give rise to pain, illness, disease, depression, obsession, and other emotional and physical problems.

Energy is often likened to a horse and attention to the rider. The horse carries the rider, but the rider can direct the horse. In spiritual practice, attention is used to direct the movement of energy—straightening the knots in the energy channels, removing the constrictions, and dissolving the blocks. When the natural flow of energy is restored, the result is clarity, balance, and understanding in mind, and health and well-being in the body.

The Tibetan tradition is full of dramatic accounts of extraordinary practices and amazing feats of endurance. My principal teacher Kalu Rinpoche, for instance, dwelt for many years in a shallow cave on the north face of a mountain, living on nothing but a sack of roasted barley and tea. One winter the weather was so cold and the snows so heavy that his family gave him up for dead. When his nephew climbed through the drifts in the early spring to see what remained of him, he was surprised to find his uncle alive and well, showing no signs of privation or difficulty. To his nephew, even in the spring the cave was a god-forsaken place, bleak and cold, with virtually no shelter from the wind. He couldn't imagine spending a single night there, let alone a whole winter. But my teacher was able to stay there without hardship. He left only when his own teacher insisted that he take over as the retreat director of the three-year retreat center at Palpung Monastery, the principal Kagyu monastery in Eastern Tibet.

How people experience energy and energy practices varies widely. During my second three-year retreat, I had several conversations with the senior chant leader from Palpung monastery. He described how, after his own three-year retreat, he ran into energy imbalances when practicing *tumo*, or inner heat. He returned to the retreat center, not to do tumo, but to do a purification practice based on Vairocana Buddha. He recited the associated mantra day and night. Even so, his condition steadily worsened. He was unable to eat or drink anything more than a small ball of roasted barley and a few sips of weak tea. He lost so much weight that he was reduced to skin and bones. His hair fell out and his fingernails fell off. He thought that even if he died, purification practice was probably the best way to meet his death, and he gave himself to the practice. His condition continued unchanged for several months. Then something did change, though he was never able to say what. He began to be able eat again, though only small quantities at first. His hair and fingernails started to regrow, and he gradually recovered his health and well-being. Afterwards, he felt a vitality that he had not known before and he was able to do tumo and other high-level energy practices without difficulty.

Personal Experience

In the three-year retreat, I studied and practiced three different traditions of high-level energy transformation methods. Probably the most well-known is the Six Practices of Naropa. Naropa was a senior scholar at the monastic university of Nalanda in the 11th century who left his position to pursue mystical practice under the guidance of Tilopa, a mystic who lived on the margins of society. The six practices are tumo (inner heat), magical apparition (illusory body), dream, sheer clarity (clear light), transference (*phowa*), and bardo (the intermediate state between death and birth). I also learned the Six Practices of Niguma, the same Niguma as in the teacher-union practice, and the Six Practices of Sukhasiddhi, another Indian mystic who took Khyungpo Naljor under her wing and taught him her own path of awakening. The differences in approach and emphasis gave me a better understanding of how these practices work and how they work with each other.

In each of these traditions, the primary energy practice is tumo. Through meditation on channels, energy, and vital essences along with breath retention practices and physical exercises, the energies of the body, particularly sexual energy, are transformed first into heat, and then into bliss. The bliss is combined with emptiness to bring about a deep experience and understanding of mind nature. The energy developed through tumo is then used to power the other practices, particularly magical apparition, dream, and sheer clarity. It was my teacher's mastery of these practices that enabled him to live without difficulty high in the mountains of Eastern Tibet.

My own experience with these practices was a bit different. In my first retreat, signs that I was on the right track soon appeared— dreams of fire and water in the case of tumo, and recognition of dreams and some ability to change them in the case of dream practice. Those small indications of effective practice were encouraging, but I knew that I had only scratched the surface. I looked forward to continuing those practices in my second three-year retreat. My enthusiasm was short-lived. In the first retreat, I had already started having digestive problems, probably induced by the mantra recitation in deity practice. Now I encountered more serious emotional and physical problems—depression, painful gastrointestinal disorders, and loss of energy and stamina. I persevered as best I could, but eventually my whole system collapsed and I could not continue with these practices. But the problems did not go away. The remaining two years of the retreat were quite difficult. By the third year, it was clear to both my teacher and me that long-term retreat was no longer a possibility for me.

After the retreat ended in 1983 I sought treatment from every possible source—Western allopathy, herbal remedies, naturopathy, homeopathy, acupuncture, massage, and so on. I went to two Tibetan doctors, thinking they might help, but to no avail. The pain in my abdomen was so intense that I often thought I needed surgery. Both my own teacher through divination and Western doctors through examinations told me unambiguously that surgery was not called for and would not help. I met a number of therapists and counsellors for help with emotional and psychological issues, but none of them could help me in any substantial way. Eventually, I consulted a Tibetan doctor I had known before entering the three-year retreats. After examining me, he said that fasting was not good for me, that acupuncture would not help, and my physiology was unsuited for breath retention practices such as tumo.

His advice confirmed what I had been forced to conclude from my own experience, and it meant I had to accept that a large body of my training was now off limits to me. While the Six Practices of Niguma provided an alternative to tumo through the triad of magical apparition, dream, and sheer clarity, depression so darkened my mind that I could rarely remember dreams, let alone recognize that I was dreaming. The pain and tension in my body made sheer clarity and other practices that depend on deep relaxation inaccessible. Even a small amount of mantra recitation triggered problems and I had to let that go, too. Any intensive practice was out, even short-term retreats. Anything more than half an hour a day and I ran into problems. In the end, I relied principally on Mahayana Mind Training and taking and sending. That practice covered all the essentials and it was the one practice that did not exacerbate my problems.

In 1985, I moved to Los Angeles to be the resident teacher of Kalu Rinpoche's center there. My physical frailty and emotional fragility limited my ability to teach and work with students. About two years later, a person who had originally come to study with me offered to teach me tai chi. My curiosity was aroused as he seemed to know a lot more than he was revealing. From him I learned tai chi and some qi gong. As it turned out, his training was primarily in the Gurdjieff tradition and martial arts. Gradually, we came to appreciate that each of us held the key to where the other was stuck. Over twelve years of meeting weekly, I taught him everything I had studied and learned, and he taught me all that he knew. It was a rich exchange.

At first, I did not notice much benefit from the tai chi and qi gong, but I kept at it. My digestive problems slowly lessened, my energy improved, and I became less fragile. It took many years and more than a few setbacks, but my condition gradually improved.

In 2003, Tsultrim Allione invited me to a Dzogchen retreat with Kilung Rinpoche. She kindly housed me in a cabin where I could practice as much or as little as mind and body allowed. The retreat proved to be a turning point. I was able to do a modest amount of practice over an extended period for the first time in twenty years. Three or four years later, during my regular morning practice, I was able to open to some deeply painful internal material. Though excruciating both physically and emotionally, the pain seemed to be a pain that wanted to be felt. By now I had quite a bit of experience in meeting internal material and I knew how to maintain balance in the process—when to stay the course, so to speak, and when not to push deeper. That day, I stayed with it for what seemed like an eternity.

Something shifted. Exactly what, I cannot say. For years, I had experienced a particular sensation, an unpleasant tingling at a specific point in my abdomen, as if energy was draining out of my body. Now that sensation was gone. Bewildered, yet grateful, I began to regain a sense of balance. While I still had to be careful about what and how much I practiced, there was little doubt that healing had begun. That experience led me to conclude that at the core of most energy imbalances are deep-seated emotional reactions that release only when experienced in open awareness.

For many years I was deeply depressed and more than a little bitter about my physical and emotional difficulties. Yet the energy imbalances forced me to pay attention to my body, to learn how to work with energy, and to learn how to rest in what arose in experience, however difficult or painful it might be. That ability, in turn, made it possible for these imbalances to resolve themselves over time. Because of the difficulties I experienced, I now take this opportunity to pass on what I learned about working with energy. It may be helpful to you or to someone you know.

Necessity

All spiritual practices involve energy transformation, from basic mindfulness to the four immeasurables, from prayer and devotion to insight, from deity practice to mantra practice and on up to high-level energy transformation practices such as tumo, magical apparition, and *tögal* (an advanced Dzogchen practice).

Difficulties and challenges posed by internal material may arise as emotional or psychological blocks, as problematic behaviors, as physical or emotional imbalances. They may arise as visitations or possession by demons and other spirits, or as visitations of protectors or dakinis. They may arise as external forces that create medical, psychological, financial, social, or existential problems; as energy or psychic imbalances that deplete mind and body; or as the idiosyncrasies of one's own mind. However they arise, they cannot be ignored.

Some form of energy practice is usually needed to develop the levels of stability and clarity in attention that make it possible to meet deeply conditioned emotional reactions and belief structures. Only through those higher levels of attention was I able to meet the difficulties I experienced. They helped to create the conditions in which the energy imbalances and physical problems could resolve themselves.

Guidance

Very few people know on their own how to work with energy practices and the problems that they may encounter. You need guidance from someone who knows the practice you are doing, how that system of practice works, and how to address imbalances in that system. Unfortunately, in the three-year retreat, I did not have access to such guidance.

Suitability

Powerful energy transformation methods such as tumo (inner heat) are not suitable for everyone. For some people, energy practice comes easily and naturally. For others, it is difficult and painful. It also depends on the system. Some work better for some people than others. To learn these practices, you need a teacher who has actual experience with them and understands how to adapt them to your physiology, suitability, and capability.

As I practiced the system my friend taught me, the energy imbalances I was experiencing gradually resolved themselves. Even with this system, I could do only a third of the amount of practice usually recommended. From all this I learned that whatever the energy system, it has to be adapted to the individual. In my case, I did better with consistent small efforts, no matter how slowly they might work.

Dangers

Energy transformation is dangerous. Devotion, for instance, can reinforce dysfunctional family patterns, particularly parental projection. Meditative absorptions (the dhyanas) can lead to addiction to experiences of bliss, clarity, or non-thought. Mantra recitation can generate its own set of energy disorders, some of which cause serious physical and mental health problems in practitioners.

When you raise energy in your mind and body, higher levels of energy activate everything, including what has been ignored or suppressed. You have no idea what you will encounter. Old behaviors, old patterns, old memories, or old karma may be stirred up. Imbalances may arise. In traditional teaching, these disturbances are described as problems with demons, as knots in the channels, as imbalance in energies, or as old karma coming to fruition. However you experience them, however you view them, they have to be met appropriately, or you run the danger of death, paralysis, or insanity. In my case, for over two decades I lived with persistent physical discomfort, recurrent bouts of intense pain, confusion, and depression, and overall diminished capacity and ability.

Balance

Another key point is balance. Every effort needs to be made to keep your system in or close to balance. Balance is the optimal condition for internal material to resolve itself and release. Too much energy, too much effort, or the wrong kind of effort causes material to arise before you have developed the ability to meet it. Too little energy, too little effort, or the wrong kind of effort lets reactive patterns take over.

Take note that balance is impossible to maintain. Try standing on one foot without moving at all. You can, however, learn to make small adjustments with increasing precision. If you train deeply, those adjustments become automatic and you remain in balance for increasing periods of time, just as you do when riding a bicycle. In this way, you create the conditions for energy to penetrate internal material and for that internal material to sort itself out and let go.

Dissolving blocks

When you are leading energy through channels or letting energy circulate in the body and you feel a block in the flow of energy, you may focus attention on where you feel the block. This approach, as I learned, is counterproductive. When you focus energy on the block, you lead energy into the block, making it worse. Here is where you need to know the natural flows of energy in the mind-body system. Instead of placing attention on the block, note the direction in which the energy would flow naturally, and place your attention a couple of inches on the other side of the block.

In this way, you lead energy through the block. If you don't know the direction of energy flow, then open to everything you experience in your body, from the crown of your head to the soles of your feet, from deep within to about two inches outside the surface of your skin. Hold your whole body in a field of attention, including the experience of the block, but not focusing on it. This method will also help to let energy flow through the block.

Practice must be regular and consistent, a gradual building of momentum rather than a dramatic effort to break through a block or problem. It may take time, but as energy moves through the block, the block begins to dissolve. As it dissolves, you may experience physical or emotional pain, memories, disturbing dreams, hallucinations, or forces, demons, or spirits moving out of you. Whatever experiences arise, let them come and go. Don't react to them. Don't suppress them. Don't try to control them. As such material starts to surface, do what you can to keep things in balance. Nourishing foods, meat, and alcohol may help (although alcohol presents its own dangers). As I wrote above, balance is the optimal condition for energy blocks to release themselves.

Release of internal material

The release of internal material typically involves four steps. The first step is to meet the internal material, however it arises, without any attempt to edit, manipulate, or control it. The second is to open to it as much as possible. This step often takes time. You have to stay in the material without being taken over by it and without suppressing it.

The third step is to experience it for what it is — movement in mind, the play of mind nature, the dance of what is. This step can be quite difficult as it involves a fundamental change in your relationship with the internal material. I needed to develop a combination of quiet determination, patience without resignation, and a willingness to let go of control. Other practitioners have compared it to the process a caterpillar goes through before becoming a butterfly. You cannot make this step happen, any more than you can make a flower bloom. It happens in its own time.

The fourth step is to stay with and in that experience and develop the ability to experience it without being conditioned by it. Freedom is not a state. It is the ability to stand in and experience what arises without falling into reactivity or confusion.

These four steps may take place over a few minutes, or they may take years to play out. In my case, they took years and involved many ups and downs and blind alleys.

While internal material is sorting itself out and your relationship with it is changing, you may feel physical pains that seem to come out of nowhere. You may have disturbing and upsetting memories. You may be gripped by fear or anger or other strong emotions for no apparent reason. Such experiences arise from the material that has been locked up or from the release of energy as the pattern breaks up. If you are not familiar with the general sequence of experiences that arise when patterns release, you may well feel that something has gone terribly wrong. Whatever you experience, make an effort to stay in balance as best you can and ride out the ups and downs. Work with it as you would anything else, as movement in mind — experiencing it, but not being consumed by it.

Splitting

Another cautionary note: perhaps better not to start, but once started, better to finish. This Tibetan saying applies to spiritual practice in general and energy transformation in particular. The point of consistent practice is to build momentum. If you have practiced consistently for five or more years, you have probably set energy transformation in motion and built some momentum. This is good. As energy transforms in your system, your attention naturally becomes clearer and more stable, and you are capable of deeper and deeper levels of insight, compassion, and understanding. If, however, you stop spiritual practice, the energy transformation that has been initiated may not stop. It usually continues on its own. One consequence is that you now have higher levels of energy in your system but you have stopped the practice that directs energy into attention and awareness.

Energy still flows through your system and activates everything, including what you ignore and suppress. Idiosyncratic behaviors and other problems may emerge, including obsessions with money, sex, or power. Without the ethics and discipline of spiritual practice, these behaviors may run amok, or you may try to suppress them. In the latter case, as I mentioned in the section on mantra, sooner or later you will find yourself being torn in two, one part acting idiosyncratically, the other part trying to suppress the idiosyncratic behavior. Perhaps better not to start, but once started, better to finish.

Ending

If you do decide to end energy practice, you can minimize the likelihood of problems by tapering off slowly. Gradually decrease the amount of time you spend doing energy practices, reducing it by a few minutes each day over a period of two or three months. The gradual decrease allows the momentum of energy practice to dissipate gradually. It also allows your body and mind to adjust to functioning without it.

When my system collapsed in the second three-year retreat, I just stopped. I had pushed too hard and I was too sick to be able to taper off gradually. The energy in my system was not dispersed in a balanced way. It stagnated instead, largely in my abdomen where it attacked the gastrointestinal system. I also suffered from depression and other problems that were clearly linked to the gastrointestinal difficulties. Several acupuncturists correctly diagnosed stagnant energy in the abdomen as the genesis of my problems, but none of them were able to treat it. Only through many years of careful energy practice — careful in the sense that I kept my mind-body system in balance and did not try to do too much too quickly — did the stagnant energy start to move and disperse.

Some of the effects of those energy imbalances have not gone away completely and probably never will. Still, what I learned has been immensely valuable, both to myself and to the people who have studied with me.

CHAPTER 7

Protector and Balance

In 1975 I did my first solo deity retreat. Kalu Rinpoche had given a small group of us the complete cycle of empowerments in the Shangpa tradition. I was drawn to a practice called *Deities of the Five Tantras* and prepared to do a one-month retreat on it. Along with meditation instructions for the practice, Rinpoche told me to do an offering ritual for the Six-Armed Mahakala every evening. Up to this point I had focused on sutra practice, groundwork, and Chenrezi meditation and I was only vaguely aware of Mahakala, the principal protector in the Shangpa lineage.

When I asked Rinpoche for instruction in Mahakala practice, he said, "You don't need it right now. Just do the ritual." He told his assistant to teach me how to do the ritual and when and how to offer the torma. I didn't even know what a torma was. Tormas are offering cakes, usually made of butter and flour, with prescribed shapes and decorations. Because I did not know how to make tormas, I was told to use cookies instead. I received no instruction in Mahakala practice, in either the meditation or the meaning of the text. Long and unpronounceable mantras were interspersed throughout the text and I had no idea what they meant. For Rinpoche none of that mattered. All that was important was for me to do the offering ritual every evening. The protectors would understand.

Later, in the three-year retreat, I did the same daily offering ritual every evening with the other retreatants and spent a full month on the associated practices—generating good fortune and prosperity, clearing away the distortions of reactivity and confusion, developing power over demons and other forces, drawing in spiritual energy and blessings, and warding off harm and difficulties. As I learned these practices and meditations, the symbolism and what everything meant, the different shrine arrangements, and the shapes and decorations for different tormas, I came to appreciate the depth and power of the magic they invoked. Still, Rinpoche's initial instruction had left an impression on me—in the world of protectors and magic, whether or not you know all the technical details or understand the symbolism, you can still honor the gods through ritual.

Protectors are the stuff of nightmares, gruesome, fearsome, even frightening—yet fascinating, too. They are clad in tiger-skin shawls, elephant-hide skirts, sorcerer's robes, bone ornaments, skull-crowns, snake-jewelry, and garlands of bloody severed heads. They hold weapons and tools—choppers, nooses, axes, death sticks, and bags of pestilence, and so on. They are usually dark red, dark blue, or black, with flaming red hair, bloodshot eyes, and bared canines. They ride rabid bears, snake-eating hawks, and mad horses. They are associated with charnel grounds and other frightening places. They reflect chthonic forces that operate deep in our psyche—dark powers that shape how we live and ways of knowing of which we are usually unaware. The protectors provide a way to connect with these forces, nourish the wakefulness inherent in them, and balance these energies in mind. You may never get used to the wrath, energy, and power of the protectors, but you do come to appreciate that your protector, however demanding and challenging he or she may be, is also the embodiment of compassion, caring for you and seeing you through the difficulties you face on your journey.

You may regard the protectors, like the dieties, as entities in their own right, living outside the scope of ordinary perception. You may also regard them as symbols or representations of structures and dynamics that are deeply encoded in body and mind, having evolved over thousands, if not millions, of years. Or you may regard them as basic energies, indefinable, ineffable, but potent sources of power on which you can draw. However you regard them, you have to relate to them even though you cannot control them. One way is through ritual. Another is through sacrifice. A third is through submission.

Using a short daily ritual for the Six-Armed Mahakala as a basis, you now learn how to practice these three principles. The ritual text itself was written by the 17th century scholar and master Taranatha. He wrote only the main part of the ritual, omitting the opening and closing sections. (Such omissions are quite common because all formal practice in the Tibetan tradition uses a tripartite structure: opening, body, and closing.) For the whole text, please see the appendices.

For the opening section, here is a short prayer written by Atisha in the 11th century. It is used in every tradition of Tibetan Buddhism:

Until I awaken, I take refuge
In Buddha, Dharma, and the Supreme Assembly.
Through the goodness of generosity and other virtues
May I awaken fully in order to help all beings.

The body of the ritual begins with the consecration of the torma offering.

Torma Blessing

FROM THE PRACTICE TEXT:

Charge the inner offerings and tormas as in deity practice.

om vajra amrita kundali hana hana hūm phat
om svabhava shuddha sarva dharma svabhava shuddho ham

In empty presence, the syllable *yam* appears and turns into wind and *ram* into fire. Above them, *ah* becomes a skull cup filled with the five meats and five elixers and the syllables *hūm, bhrum, ām, dzring,* and *kham.* Winds blow, fires blaze, and the ten substances along with the syllables melt together. I draw and mix in the elixir of awareness from the hearts of all buddhas, creating a great sea of liquid timeless awareness.

om ah hūm ha ho hri

Repeat three times

INSTRUCTION:

With the first spell—*om vajra amrita…*—you charge an ancient Indian god, Vajra Amrita, to clear a space for the consecration. With the second spell—all experience is utterly pure, I am utterly pure—conceptual thinking drops away. Your mind takes form as a giant cauldron fashioned from the top of a human skull. It rests on a hearth of three other skulls, blazing with the fires and fanned by the winds at the end of time.

This cauldron contains reactivity and confusion (the five meats and the five elixirs), the five aspects of awakening, and the five aspects of timeless awareness. Heated by the winds and fires, all these ingredients melt together to form a sea of radiant clear elixir. A blue-black letter *hūm* appears above it, radiates light, and draws in the timeless awareness and energy of buddhas everywhere. The skull cauldron is filled with a sea of liquid timeless awareness. Consecrate this offering with the seed syllables of the five aspects of timeless awareness.

◇◇◇

Even after all these years I still cannot read this torma blessing without thinking of the three witches in Shakespeare's *Macbeth*:

Double, double, toil and trouble;
Fire burn, and cauldron bubble

Are you, like the witches, preparing a magical brew from human flesh, dog and horse meat, urine, feces, menstrual blood, and semen? Are you acting out a symbolic drama of transformation in which these symbols of reactivity and confusion melt in a cauldron that itself is the union of bliss and emptiness? Are you drawing on a higher level of energy, invoking the wind of energy to fan the inner fire of understanding and generate a level of energy and attention that helps you meet the challenges of spiritual practice? In some mysterious way, this consecration ritual speaks of the transformation that takes place when you rest clear and present in the depths of confusion and reactivity.

Connection-being

FROM THE PRACTICE TEXT:

om svabhava shuddha sarva dharma svabhava shuddho ham

In empty presence, in front of me, on a lotus and sun, *hūm* appears and turns into the Six-Armed Lord of Timeless Awareness, his body blue-black in color. His first pair of hands hold a chopper and skull cup, the second pair a rosary of human heads and a trident, and the last a hand-drum and noose. He wears a tiger-skin skirt, bone and snake jewelry, a necklace of severed heads, and sets of bells on his arms and legs. His two legs support him in the balanced posture and crush Obstacle-Maker. He has three eyes and bared fangs. His beard, eyebrows, and hair flare upwards. He is crowned by Buddha Unshakeable and bears a drop of cinnabar on his forehead. He stands in the middle of a blazing mass of fire, his back against the trunk of a sandalwood tree.

On his left, from the syllable *bhyo* arises Shri Devi, black, riding a mule and holding a demon stick and a bag of pestilence. In front is Malefactor Kshetrapala, dark brown, holding a chopper and skull cup, riding a rabid black bear. On the right is Jinamitra, reddish black, holding a hand-drum and wheel. Behind is Takkiraja, black, holding a razor and skull cup filled with blood. On the left is Demon Lord Trakshé, holding a battle standard and skull cup containing a human heart, riding a black demon horse with white fetlocks, and wearing a flowing silk cape and felt boots.

Around them throng the seventy-five glorious lords and a sea of oath-bound protectors.

Cast the spell that dispels the enchantment of the conceptual mind. Instantly become your meditation deity. In front of you, your mind takes form as the Six-Armed Lord and his entourage. His blue-black body towers over you. He glares at you through three bloodshot eyes as he gnashes his monstrous canines. The roar of his rage fills the universe as his six arms slash the air with hideous implements. His feet trample on Obstacle-Maker, who spews jewels from every orifice. His entourage is equally terrifying. They dance and prance in blazing fire, brandishing toothed wheels, straight razors, spears, bags of pestilence, and death sticks. One rides a rabid bear, another a demonic horse, and a third a mad mule. These are the connection-beings — your mind arising in these forms.

Awareness-being

FROM THE PRACTICE TEXT:

My heart radiates light that draws the Six-Armed Lord of Timeless Awareness from the sandalwood tree with a single trunk in the Cool Grove in the south-east, with the root and lineage gurus above, grimacing warriors on the right, smiling amazons on the left, and a horde consisting of oceans of committed protectors, local guardians, messengers, and those bound by oaths.

> *om vajra mahakala sapari wari kching*
> *kching kching kching kching*
> *kching kching kching kching*
> *kching kching kching kching*
> *kching kching kching kching*
> *kching kching kching kching*
> *vajra samaja ja hūm bam ho*

INSTRUCTION:

Light radiates from the hearts of all the beings in front of you, radiating to the furthest reaches of space and time. It summons the awareness-beings. Kching. Ankle bells jingle. Kching. More jingling. Kching, kching. The ground shakes as the primordial Lord of Awareness makes his way step by step from "the sandalwood tree with a single trunk in the Cool Grove in the south-east." A fragrance of sandalwood wafts on a slight breeze. The air around you becomes electric. The hair on the back of your neck stands up and you feel a chill up your spine. As the awareness-beings join with the connection-beings in front of you, they take on a life of their own. You have been noticed.

Offering and Praise

FROM THE PRACTICE TEXT:

> *hūm*
> This outer offering of fine heavenly things
> That arise through interdependence
> I present to the Lord and his retinue.
> Please accept them for protecting the teachings.
> *om shri mahakala sapari wari argham padyam pukpé dhupé aloké gendhé névidya shapda praticha hūm svaha*
>
> *om ah hūm*
>
> Although you do not move from the realm of totality
> You take a wrathful form to subdue evil.
> You who destroy the enemies of the teachings,
> Great Black One, I bow to you.

Greet the Great Black Lord, his attendants, and his entourage as you would any important guest arriving from a long journey. Proffer the traditional offerings: water to drink, water to wash with, flowers, incense, light, perfume, food, and music, along with bowls of elixir and hymns of praise. From your heart send out gods and goddesses with all these offerings, and offer them to the assembly before you.

Now practice three ritual elements: engaging obligation, mantra recitation, and torma offering. Practice as if you are dreaming — knowing that everything you experience is your own mind, yet at the same time it has a vitality and life of its own.

Engaging Obligation

FROM THE PRACTICE TEXT:

Obligation gifts as vast as the offering clouds of
    Ever-present Good appear.
om vajra spharana kham

hūm

Fast-acting compassion, All Seeing One,
Great Black One with six arms,
Lord of energy and your retinue,
I'm here to engage your terrifying obligations.

All the riches of the world and everything in it
Arise naturally as clouds of wonderful offerings.
Treasures from fearful charnel grounds
Where evil forces were destroyed are spread all around.

The power of this contemplative's devotion magnifies
The commitment offerings enjoyed in the great mysteries.
With these offerings,
I sate your incomprehensible desires—

Ravens that soar like garudas,
Fleet horses and majestic yaks,
Graceful sheep and fierce dogs,
The thirteen-fold black offerings bedecked with ribbons
        and jewels,

Magic arrows adorned with silks and mirrors,
Knifed hearts packed with soul stones and spells,
Seas of medicine-juice and blood,
Mountains of sacrificial and power offerings,

And especially, mind itself, utter simplicity,
Single-minded faith and devotion
In the guru and the lord, inseparable.

Receive these offerings
Lord of Pristine Awareness, Wish-granting Gem,
In all the forms you assume,

Along with Lady Glorious Goddess,
Malefactor, Force, Death Lord, and Demon,
And the seventy-five oath-bound and others
Surrounded by all the lordly powers of the three planes
        of existence.

Protect me from threats now, in the future, and in the
        intermediate states.
Build up my stores of food, wealth, and experience.
Make the understanding and practice of the teachings spread.
Set all beings free in full awakening.

INSTRUCTION:

Look at Mahakala and his entourage standing in a mass of fire in front of you, waiting to hear why you summoned them. Tell them, "I'm here to engage your terrifying obligations," and start presenting gifts to them. Send out gods and goddesses who give them everything you can imagine enjoying through your senses, the exquisite caress and breathtaking colors of beautiful fabrics, silk, linen, cashmere, and the finest cotton, the stunning beauty of fine paintings and sculptures, rainbows, sunsets, gardens, meadows, mountain lakes, and other magnificent sights and vistas, delicious foods that ravish the palate, fragrances that bring delight and joy, and music whose beauty cannot be put into words.

Then give Mahakala and his entourage the stuff of nightmares — treasures from the charnel grounds, the bones of seven-born saints, the relics of mystics, troops of black offerings — thirteen large powerful ravens, thirteen fierce black mastiffs, thirteen fearsome black bears, thirteen wild black stallions, thirteen black rams, scorpions, spiders, lizards, and snakes.

To these two sets of offerings, now add the stuff of sorcery — magic wands, magic arrows, hearts taken from the corpses of murderers and stuffed with precious stones and powerful spells, medicines, cordials, and elixirs, charged stones and knives, and magic powders concocted by sorcerers.

Offer all of this to your teacher and lord, seeing your teacher and Mahakala as not different. Make these offerings with you as your meditation deity. Let these offerings arise magically out of your devotion, without thought or concept.

Then charge Mahakala and his entourage to fulfill their obligations, namely, to create the conditions that wake you up and to dispel the situations that keep you asleep.

◇◇◇

Outer offerings pertain to the five senses. When you offer sensory enjoyment that you would normally attach to, your investment in sensory enjoyment is gradually eroded. You become more able to enjoy the sights, sounds, tastes, smells, and textures of the world without needing to make them yours. This level of offering corresponds to the first empowerment, the vase empowerment, eroding the seeming solidity of what you experience through your senses.

Inner offerings pertain to emotional reactivity. Over time, offering the stuff of nightmares changes your relationship with emotional reactivity. It loses its solidity and you are increasingly able to experience emotional reactions as reactions without being taken over by them. In this way, inner offerings correspond to the second empowerment, the secret empowerment.

The secret offerings are the dark forces that shape your life and the lives of others, forces that operate without thought, doing whatever they have to do — ensuring your survival, for instance, or helping you follow your calling. As you touch those forces through these offerings, your relationship with them gradually changes, bringing you to the point that you are able to recognize and experience them as movements in mind, rather than something that just takes over in you. These secret offerings correspond to the third empowerment, the wisdom-awareness empowerment.

The mystical offering is the utter simplicity of mind itself and corresponds to the fourth empowerment.

◇◇◇

Initially, I had a lot of difficulty in understanding exactly what engaging obligation was about. The Tibetan term *thugs dam bskang* (pron. tūk dam kong) was unfamiliar to me. When I asked my teacher about it, he replied, "Suppose you want an important person to do something for you. You invite him to your home, you serve him a sumptuous meal, you entertain him with music and dance, and you give him valuable gifts. Then, when he is relaxed and happy, you ask him to do what you want him to do. Because you have fed and entertained him, given him gifts and praised him, he is obliged to help you."

At the time what struck me most was that the relationship with the protectors was brazenly transactional. When I make these offerings to Mahakala, I oblige him to take care of me. Later, however, I came to understand that Rinpoche had told me only half the story. The other half I had to discover myself.

Mantra Recitation

FROM THE PRACTICE TEXT:

> *om vajra mahakala kching chetra vighana vinayaka hūm hūm pāt*
> *pāt svaha*

INSTRUCTION:

Start reciting Mahakala's mantra. In essence it is a spell that calls upon Mahakala to eliminate any and all obstacles to your awakening. The syllables of the mantra rise from your heart like wisps of smoke. They form a chain of black letters that radiate red light and carry the energy of your devotion. The chain comes out of your mouth, enters Mahakala's mouth, and goes down to his heart. Let the mantra chain carry your devotion right into Mahakala's heart.

The mantra chain continues inside Mahakala down to his power center at the level of the navel, exits from his form, enters your body through your navel, and comes up to your heart, completing the circle. The mantra chain carries Mahakala's energy and capabilities and brings his wrath, compassion, and power into your navel and into your heart.

Recite the mantra steadily while the mantra chain carries your faith and devotion to Mahakala and brings his power and energy into you.

◇◇◇

When you grow tired from practice, you lose connection with the empty clarity of mind nature, you lapse into thinking your way through this practice, and try to visualize everything instead. This is counterproductive in three ways. You reinforce conceptual experience, waste effort in visualization, and generate energy imbalances.

Instead, when you notice that you have lapsed into thinking or visualizing, let everything drop. Let your mind go empty and rest. Say the mantra softly and slowly, as a way to rest mind and body. When you feel refreshed and restored and back in balance, let the presence of Mahakala arise again in your mind, like a rainbow forming in a clear sky. Let the mantra circulation arise in the same way. Feel Mahakala's power and energy filling your whole being, refreshing you, restoring balance, and reconnecting you with the empty clarity of your own mind.

Torma Offering

FROM THE PRACTICE TEXT:

Add *idam balingta kha kha khahi khahi* to the end of Mahakala's mantra and repeat three times.

Likewise, add *idam balingta kha kha khahi khahi* to the end of each of:

> *bhyo mamo nakmo vitali sindha kulu kulu hūm pāt*
> *om chetra pala vighana hūm pāt*
> *om jina mitra vasham kuru hūm pāt*
> *om traki raja samaya bhyo du dza hūm pāt*
> *om du yog dza mahakala traraksha hūm pāt*

repeating each of them three times.

Then repeat

> *om shri mahakalaya shasanam upakarinam éshapashima kaloyam*
> *idam ratna trayaya apakarinam yatipratjnya samara satada idam*
> *duktram kha kha khahi khahi mara mara grihana grihana pendha*
> *pendha hana hana daha daha pacha pacha dinamekena maraya*
> *hūm pāt*

three times with *idam balingta kha kha khahi khahi* to offer the torma to the host of oath-bound protectors.

> *argham padyam pukpé dhupé aloké gendhé névidya shapda praticha*
> *hūm svaha*

With

> *om ah hūm*

present the inner offering.

> *hūm*
> I bow to fast-acting All Seeing One.
> Your feet, graced with anklets, crush Obstacle-Maker.
> Great Black One, wearing a tiger-skin skirt,
> Your six arms are decorated with snake ornaments.
>
> Your first right holds a chopper, the next a rosary,
> And the last violently rattles a hand-drum.
> Your left hands hold a skull cup, a trident,
> And a noose for catching and binding.
>
> Your face is contorted in wrath, your canines fully bared,
> With three fearsome eyes, and hair flaring upwards.
> Your forehead is marked with a drop of cinnabar
> And Buddha Unshakeable, on your head, is your seal.
>
> You wear a necklace of fifty human heads dripping with blood
> And a crown of five skulls inlaid with jewels.
> Come from your grove and take these sacrificial offerings.
> Please accept this offered sacrifice,
>
> And to my companions and me
> Give health, strong lives, and power,
> Glory, fame, and good fortune,
> And property, wealth, and vast riches.

Give us mastery in pacification
Enrichment and other activities.
Keep your commitments and protect us.
Use your abilities and support us.

Eliminate untimely death, illness,
Emotional disturbances, and impediments.
Bad dreams, bad omens,
Bad business, eliminate them all.

Make the world happy, crops grow,
Harvests full, and the Dharma flourish.
Make everything wonderful and joyous;
Bring about all that we wish for.

INSTRUCTION:

To offer the torma itself, make the offering gesture, a bowl formed by interlacing your fingers and cupping your hands. For each of the three repetitions, form the bowl and repeat the mantras as directed in the practice text. The added Sanskrit phrase means "eat, eat, eat this cake."

Recall the torma you prepared at the beginning of this ceremony—a skull cauldron filled with liquid timeless awareness. It now magically appears in front of you. Through straws made from light the protectors drink the timeless awareness. Nourished, their forms grow brighter and brighter. Fortified, they grow larger and more menacing. Sated, they stand ready and waiting to do your bidding.

Make the traditional celebratory offerings and praise them. Then make your requests. Ask them to act on your behalf. In response, Mahakala and his entourage stomp and rage, emitting thousands of forms of themselves like sparks from a sparkler. These forms fly to the furthest corners of the universe, calming what needs to be calmed, enriching and expanding what needs to be enriched, compelling what resists resolution, and bringing an end to what has to be let go.

Charge them with calming the problems that keep you from practicing effectively—illness, emotional disturbances, interruptions, internal or external obstacles or blocks, threats from enemies, problems, or difficulties in the lives of those close to you or who depend on you, and so on. If you are experiencing difficulties, tell them to give you strength, vitality, good fortune, better food, better living conditions, or the right medicines or treatments. Tell them to increase the resources available to you and to others—time, money, manpower, strategy, connections, or influence. If your problems persist, then charge the protectors to compel a resolution by exercising their power and charisma to charm, seduce, intimidate, or threaten the powers and forces responsible, whether they are human or non-human, spiritual or secular, sentient or non-sentient, natural or man-made. Finally, if compelling fails, charge them to bring an end to the problem—by freeing you from your relationship with the problem, or by removing them or you from the problem.

◇◇◇

Whatever these dark forces are, however you view or understand them, in this ritual you nourish them with timeless awareness. While this ritual probably evolved from actual sacrifices, the only sacrifice here is your reactivity and confusion. Placed in the skull cauldron that is the union of bliss and emptiness, melted by the fires of the end of time, and then combined with the potentials of awakening, your reactivity and confusion become a shining sea of timeless awareness. As you nourish the protectors with timeless awareness, you establish the conditions that make it possible for you to experience your darkest reactions and murkiest confusion in clear open awareness. That experience changes your relationship with those patterns. They cease to be forces to be feared and avoided. They become movements of your own mind, full of power and potential.

Conclusion

FROM THE PRACTICE TEXT:

Guru and Lord, inseparable,
In you I earnestly take refuge.
May I clear away
Every reaction in every being.

Lord and Guru, inseparable,
In you I earnestly take refuge.
May I clear away
Every impediment for every being.

Repeat three times

Repeat the hundred-syllable mantra three times and the apology prayers.

Whatever mistakes I've made
In mantras, rituals, or activities
Profound and perfect as you are,
I ask you to bear them patiently.

INSTRUCTION:

Conclude with the customary closures. Acknowledge that your performance of the ritual has not been perfect. Ask the protectors to be patient with your mistakes. Then send them back to their respective abodes. Alternatively, my teacher taught to let the protector and the entourage dissolve into light and then let that light come into your heart. This instruction serves two purposes: it reminds you that everything you experience is mind and it plants the energy of the protector in you. Carry the energy of the protector with you as you go about your day. Whatever happens to you, good or bad, see it as the activity of the protector, pointing you to the mystery of life.

As with all rituals in the Tibetan tradition, conclude with dedication, aspiration, and good fortune prayers. The text does not include any specific ones.

Ritual, Sacrifice, and Submission

Protector practice works on at least three levels simultaneously. The rituals of protector practice are magic deployed for mystical purposes — a framework and structure refined over hundreds of years aimed at leading you into the mystery of life. The drama of the ritual speaks to deeper emotional levels in you, yearnings to know the mystery directly. As you become aware of those yearnings, you sacrifice the illusion of control to the mystery of life itself. The metaphors and symbols in protector practice resonate with still deeper levels and attune your whole being to mystical insights and experiences, a resonance that allows you to submit to the unfolding of understanding in your being.

Ritual

Protector rituals are magic. They are a way to direct attention, intention, and will to effect change in you and change in the world you experience. You create the presence of the protector and invite the primordial protector to join with your creation. You pray and make offerings, asking the protector to act on your behalf. You use sigils and spells, seed syllables and mantras, to circulate energy. You nourish the protector, make more offerings, and charge the protector to act as he or she sees fit — calmly, expansively, powerfully, or forcefully.

And something happens. Over time those ritual elements transform how you experience the world, both in terms of what happens inside you and what happens around you. You have dreams or visions. You have intuitions as to what to do even though they make little rational sense. You become sensitive to signs and omens. You uncover a peace and a clarity that enable you to see situations differently. Or something out of the blue happens and your life changes irrevocably in ways that you never anticipated.

Magic is unpredictable. When you exercise magic, you are not in control. You project your will into the world, and the world responds in its own way. What happens may not be what you had in mind, but as time unfolds it may turn out to be exactly what you needed.

Sacrifice

Etymologically, to sacrifice something means to make it sacred. When you practice Vajrayana, you may have to sacrifice a part or all of your life to practice. If you are not willing to sacrifice parts of your life, then Vajrayana is probably not for you. To put it another way, any part of your life may become sacred if it becomes a path through which you awaken. You do not get to choose. You do not know the patterns of conditioning that prevent you from being awake. Nor do you know what you need to wake up. Further, when you employ magic to charge the protectors to do whatever is necessary for you to wake up, you cede control over your life.

When a king sends a general to take care of a problem at the edge of his realm, both the king and the general go into the dark. Once the king has dispatched the general, the king is no longer in charge. The general is, but he does not know what he is going to find at the border. Whatever the problem, the general is obligated to address it, one way or another.

The king has no say in what the general does. The king may think that the enemies at the border need to be destroyed, but the general may broker a peace treaty instead. The king may think the troublemakers can be starved into submission, but the general resolves the border problems by providing the troublemakers with land and water to grow crops. The general may even see the king is the problem. Instead of settling the problem at the border, he turns around and deposes the king.

You are the king and the protector is your general. When you make a commitment to awakening and put the protectors in obligation to fulfill theirs, you step into the dark.

This is the other half of the story, the half that Rinpoche did not tell me. When you charge the protectors to create the conditions for you to awaken, you are implicitly acknowledging that you do not control your life and that your conscious conceptual understanding does not know what you need to wake up. From that point on what happens in your life is, in a certain sense, irrelevant. You have chosen or been chosen to enter a mystery, and it is up to you to live in it. Your commitment is to living awake. If it takes a nightmare to shake you loose from your entanglement with reactive patterns and conceptual confusion, your life may become a nightmare.

My second three-year retreat and what followed was one such nightmare. As I mentioned earlier, one of the effects of retreat practice was a serious energy imbalance that weakened me physically and mentally for many years. But that was only a part of the picture. Stubborn, arrogant, unfeeling in ways that are embarrassing to acknowledge today, contemptuous of a body that I saw simply as a vehicle for mystical pursuit, I thought I knew what I was doing and what was best for me.

The protectors did what I had charged them to do. They created the conditions I needed to wake up. They stripped away my health, my sense of capability, my pride, my reliance on intellectual understanding, and my self-respect. They shut down any possibility of intensive retreat practice and cut me off from practicing almost all the methods I had learned. And they exiled me to a small desert town in California called Los Angeles.

I was left with no choice. I had to change. I had to find a completely different approach to life and to spiritual practice. It was not easy and it took a long time. I do not look back on those times with joy, but at the same time, I am grateful. I am not sure that anything else would have led me to change.

Submission

Submission means that you live practice in whatever life brings to you. It does not mean blind obedience to an arbitrary higher power or higher authority. It means you listen, and listen deeply, without preference or prejudice, to everything going on in your life. In that field of attention you become aware of balance and imbalance, often as a tactile sensation more than as a cognitive understanding (though that may follow). However you sense imbalance, it tells you what needs attention and what needs to happen. That is what you submit to. That is one way the protectors tell you what to do.

As you spend time with these fearsome figures, you form a relationship with the dark, unreasoning, and unreasonable aspects of life and the dark, unreasoning, and unreasonable parts of your own psyche. When you encounter a truly difficult situation in life or practice, you may be surprised by how clearly you see the situation and how you know what needs to done — without recourse to the conceptual mind.

Involvement with the protectors may take place in other ways. They may take notice of you and act accordingly. Without any explicit request or understanding on your part, they generate situations in your life that bring you into mystical practice. When you resist, your life moves out of balance and becomes more difficult. When you submit, you and your life become more balanced. It makes no difference whether you see the protectors as outside entities shaping your life, as deep aspects of your psyche looking to take expression in your life, or as energies in your being seeking to resolve tensions and imbalances, the result is the same. You end up taking a path that had not occurred to you.

It may seem that I am talking about deities and protectors as external entities that act on their own. In the beginning, yes, they seemed that way to me. They seemed to embody powers and forces that I could only access through them. They seemed to be definitely other and not only other but greater, too. As I became more familiar with the protectors through this ritual, I gradually came to see that though they might be other, there was also a give and take, a reciprocal relationship that was only possible if we were in some way equals. Then I began to see that they embodied, or represented, aspects of my own mind, and I came to relate to them as expressions of mind nature, the utter groundlessness of experience. Because I did not have access to the knowing itself, I could only access it through symbols. As time passed, however, I came to see that deities and protectors are the power and activity of my own mind, doing what needs to be done to undermine the operation of reactivity, confusion, and the persistent sense of self that distorts the experience of life. Having said that, I also see that this progression, in effect the four levels of tantra as my teacher explained them to me, could begin to unfold only after any notion that I was in control had been completely and utterly taken away. Stripped bare, I had to reach out to what I did not know, and to rely on it without any hope or expectation of achievement.

Another Balancing Practice

Hail damaged the fields of barley. Then strange winds flattened the surviving crops. Unseasonable snows trapped flocks of sheep in the mountains. Avalanches threatened the men who went to rescue them. One trouble after another made life more and more difficult for a village in the mountains of Eastern Tibet.

The elders turned to the village lama for help. After doing a divination, he told them that the local god had been neglected and was showing his displeasure. The lama performed several ceremonies, but the troubles continued. The elders brought in another lama, and then another, and another — to no avail. Eventually, they asked my teacher's teacher, Lama Norbu Dondrup, for help.

When Lama Norbu arrived in the village, the elders pointed to a rocky crag on the mountain. "That's where the god dwells," they said. Lama Norbu and his attendant climbed up the mountain to a point just below the outcropping. Tired from the climb, Lama Norbu asked for some tea before he started the offering ceremonies. His attendant gathered wood, made a fire, and soon had a cup of hot buttered tea ready. Lama Norbu held the cup in his hands and said a short offering prayer to the local god. As was custom, he dipped the ring finger on his right hand into the tea and flicked a few drops of tea into the air — an offering gesture that accompanied the offering prayer.

The god's face suddenly appeared in the cup of tea. "Your offering I accept," the god said. "The other lamas were full of themselves and thought they could order me around. I ignored them. You made this offering freely, without condition. I accept it. Tell the villagers I won't cause them any more trouble." Then the god disappeared.

Balancing rituals take many forms. A burnt offering ritual is directed primarily to a category of gods and demons who create problems because they feel that they are owed something. The purpose of this ritual is to restore balance in you, in your immediate world, and in the world around you. It removes or wards off interruptions and disruptions to practice. In Tibet, these kinds of rituals were also performed to address problems with local gods and demons.

Mountain Burnt-Offering

FROM THE RITUAL TEXT:

Make a fire full of good fortune, that is, in a clean hearth or container build a fire and burn whatever you have at hand: aromatic woods, resins, medicinal plants, the white and sweet foods, incense, powders, etc. Then sprinkle water on the fire and consecrate the offerings with:

om ah hūm

INSTRUCTION:

Burnt-offering rituals primarily address troublemakers. Troublemakers belong to a class of spirits called smell-eaters. Highly reactive, quick to take offense, they inhabit a kind of in-between state in which their only sources of nourishment are smells, odors, aromas, and fragrances — hence the burning of offerings such as incense, pine needles, or juniper berries, fragrant woods such as pine, cedar, or sandalwood, and aromatic foods.

As you sprinkle consecrated water on the offerings to be burnt, repeat the three syllables *om, āh, hūm* to consecrate the offerings with the body, speech, and mind of the buddhas.

FROM THE RITUAL TEXT:

Refuge

Fierce and potent master of awareness, Pema Tötreng Tsal,
Essence of all sources of refuge in the infinity of existence
      and peace,
In your form, the mandala of buddhas in all experience,
      potential and actual, is complete.
In order to free all beings from existence, I take refuge in you.

Repeat three times.

Awakening mind

I form the intention in order that
In ground presence, the absolute mystery, the sheer clarity of
      timeless awareness,
The distortions of all beings are cleared away;
In awakened body, speech, and mind presence, the four
      visions unfold naturally,
And thus, in the youthful vase body, all beings are free.

Repeat three times.

Seven-section prayer

In being natural awareness, direct and open, I pay homage.
In being sheer clarity, limitless and unfathomable, I present
      offerings.
In being the expanse where all experience, patterned and
      free, is in balance, I confess.
In being the end of experience, beyond mind, I rejoice.

In being the great completion, naturally present, I turn the
      wheel of teaching.
In uprooting patterned existence from its depths, I pray.
In being utterly beyond thinking about the three domains,
      I dedicate.

INSTRUCTION:

The ritual begins with a short homage to the lineage, as embodied
in Guru Padmasambhava, the progenitor of the Nyingma lineage in
Tibet. Refuge and awakening mind follow, expressed in the mystical
terminology of Dzogchen. A version of the seven-section prayer follows. In this interpretation of the seven sections, each aspect of the
prayer is expressed as an activity of direct awareness.

    In explicitly mystical prayers such as these, don't try to imagine or
contrive what is being expressed. You cannot access what is beyond
concept with the conceptual mind. These prayers are poetry, pointing you to what can be experienced but cannot be put into words. Sit
empty and let the words act on you.

Generation of Self

From the unceasing energy that arises from the realm of what
      is, the originally pure,
I take form as Pema Tötreng Tsal, reddish white, in the flower
      of youth.
My form blazes with the splendor of the major and minor
      marks. I hold a vajra and skull-cup.
Handsome and majestic in robes and jewelry,
Connection- and awareness-beings combined, in form the
      union of all buddhas,
I am the great and glorious lord of samsara and nirvana.
om ah hūm vajra guru padma siddhi hūm

Repeat a hundred times.

Instantly, miraculously, you become Pema Tötreng Tsal, the form of Guru Padmasambhava associated with subduing demons who make trouble. These demons are highly reactive, erupting unpredictably with the corrosive energy of envy, jealousy, greed, or pride. They are consumed by anger, resentment, and bitterness, unable to appreciate anything good in their lives. They need to be met with a strong, no-nonsense, yet kind presence, exactly what Tötreng Tsal represents.

Repeat the Vajra Guru mantra a hundred times, letting go of your own reactivity and sense of self and connecting with the energy of Tötreng Tsal.

FROM THE RITUAL TEXT:

To purify the fire offerings:

ram yam kham

In empty presence, the fire offerings appear — huge clouds rising from oceans of pure timeless awareness, wonderfully pleasing to every sense, spreading and filling the whole sky.

Charge the fire offerings with the three syllables and three repetitions of the sky-treasure mantra.

om ah hūm
nama sarva tathagatabhyo vishvamukhebhye sarva thakham ungate
saparana emam gagana kham svaha.

Repeat three times.

INSTRUCTION:

Consecrate the offerings with *om ah hūm*. Even though in the ritual they are burnt in the fire, the consecrated offerings take on a mythic dimension and are presented to all the guests, including the troublemakers, as clouds of timeless awareness.

Multiply the offerings with the Sky Treasure Spell. As you recite the spell, the offerings spontaneously multiply, filling the sky with clouds of awareness as far as the mind can reach.

bhrūm
In large shining vessels made of precious metals and jewels
The commitment offerings, all that gives pleasure in
        this world,
Are charged with the energy of the three syllables and become
        liquid timeless awareness,
Exciting the pleasurable sensations of all experience,
        patterned and free.

This offering I present to the gurus, deities, dakinis,
        and protectors,
And all the buddha mandalas in the ten directions,
The local deities of this world, the six kinds of beings, and the
        debt-collecting guests,
Particularly those who would take my life and steal
        my energy,

The malicious elemental spirits who inflict illness
        and interruptions,
Those who send bad portents and bad omens in dreams
        and symbols,
The eight kinds of unruly demons, the masters of illusions,
Those who have come to collect food, shelter, or wealth,

The forces of darkness and madness, the shades of men and
        women dead and gone,
Ghosts of the murdered, monastery ghosts, house ghosts,
        ghouls, and vampires.
Burnt in these red flames, my debts are paid.
Pleasures rain down, giving everyone exactly what they want.

Present these offerings to the four guests who are traditionally invited to offering ceremonies: the buddhas and bodhisattvas invited out of respect, the protectors and dakinis invited because of their abilities, the six kinds of beings invited out of compassion, and the eight classes of demons invited to resolve karmic debts. The clouds of awareness that you offer fulfill the desires of all the troublemakers, quelling their bitterness and resentment and all the unresolved issues that lead them to haunt you in the small hours of the night.

FROM THE RITUAL TEXT:

> For as long as the sky is there
> I share these infinite sensory pleasures with them.
> May the bad and corrupt things I've done and will do,
> Appropriating offerings for the Jewels, for the faithful, or for
>   the dead,
>
> Be cleared away by this offering fire and burnt offerings.
> The tongues of flame touch every particle of what can be or
>   is experienced.
> May limitless clouds of offerings, as in the aspirations of
>   Ever-present Good,
> Entirely fill the domains of the awakened.
>
> These tongues of flame blaze with the offering rays of the five
>   wisdom lights.
> The light fills the six realms down to the depths of the
>   deepest hells.
> Those who go round and round in the three realms are freed
>   in rainbow-light bodies.
> May all beings wake up to their awake nature.
>
> *om ah hūm*

Repeat a hundred or a thousand times or more.

Then formulate a profound wish, that all beings, including those who cause trouble for you, be freed in timeless awareness.

Recite the offering mantra *om ah hūm* as you present these offerings again and again. You are Padmasambhava. You have infinite resources on which to draw. Please the buddhas with your offerings. Oblige the protectors to take care of you. Ease the struggles of sentient beings. And sate the ravenous appetites of the troublemakers, helping them at long last to let go of their desperation, vindictiveness, and rage and find peace.

FROM THE RITUAL TEXT:

> The three dimensions of awakening, pure in their being,
> Form the receptacle, an eternal palace of infinite space.
> In it, all the matter of the world, potential and actual,
> What is true, what is vivid, and what is there,
>
> Melts and becomes liquid awareness,
> Its blazing light filling the sky.
> The essences of this elixir, drawn from all experience,
>   patterned and free,
> I share with all who have ever been my guest
> From time without beginning until now.
>
> May we acquire the abilities of ground, path, and fruition,
> And clear away disruptions in outlook, practice, and behavior.
> In the infinite expanse of the wonderful mind of
>   Ever-present Good,
> May we take hold of eternal being in the youthful vase body.
> And when the great sea of samsara is emptied
> May we all become fully awake in the Lotus Web
>   Supreme Realm.

INSTRUCTION:

Now take the offerings to another level.

Here, all the matter of the world, that is, all experience, is transformed into liquid timeless awareness and is again offered to the four guests: those invited out of respect, because of their power, out of compassion, and because they cause trouble.

FROM THE RITUAL TEXT:

> The fire offering of heaps and elements blazes brilliantly with radiant health.
> The fire offering of white and red awakening mind blazes with bliss-emptiness.
> The fire offering of emptiness and compassion fills the totality of experience.
>
> On the ground of the five vajra lights, all experience, potential or actual, patterned or free,
> I present the fire offering of naturally present complete awakening.

INSTRUCTION:

Then make the secret and mystical offerings as above.

Having honored the gods with all these offerings—the actual burning of different kinds of foods and fragrant plants and minerals, and the inner, secret, and mystical offerings—ask for what you want and ask the gods to fulfill their responsibilities.

FROM THE RITUAL TEXT:

> Old karmic debts—may they be cleared away.
> Current breaches—I confess now so that they don't continue.
> Future clouding—may I not be caught in that cycle.

I confess all violations, conscious or unconscious
Of the vows and training
Of individual liberation, awakening being, and awareness
       holder,
And the promises connected with the secret mantra.

May illness, disturbances, distortions, and impurities be
       cleared away.
May the plagues, famines, and wars of this age be eased.

Barbarian attacks on the homeland — stop!
Interruptions to the work of teachers — stop!
Bad portents for the good of the world — stop!
Shortening of life by planets, serpents, or kingly demons —
       stop!
The eight great threats and sixteen fears — stop!
Bad fortune for me and those around me — stop!
The power and influence of commitment demons and self-
       interest demons — stop!

INSTRUCTION:

Because the burnt-offering ritual is directed primarily at trouble-makers, pray to be free of trouble:

Old karmic debts — may they be cleared away.
Current breaches — I confess now so that they don't continue.
Future clouding — may I not be caught in that cycle.

Finally, take the flat disc of the sun in your left hand and the flat disc of the moon in your right hand. Clap your hands together as you say the word "stop." When the sun and moon come together, that is, when the sun of emptiness joins with the moon of compassion, all negativity — all resentment and bitterness, all jealousy and greed, all thought of being owed or being in debt — vanishes.

Each of the seven lines ending in "stop!" has outer, inner, and mystical levels of meaning. For instance, barbarian attacks can be understood as attempts by foreign powers to put an end to any form of spiritual practice, circumstances in your life that make it difficult for you to practice, or aspects of your own mind that attack your commitment and practice discipline. In the same way, the eight great threats are lions (internally, the lion of pride), elephants (the elephant of delusion), fire (anger), snakes (envy), thieves (wrong view), chains (avarice), floods (desire), and demons (the fell demon of doubt).

FROM THE RITUAL TEXT:

> May these offerings please the buddhas.
> May they fulfill the desires of the oath-bound.
> May they meet the wants of the six kinds of beings.
> May they satisfy the owed and the resentful.
>
> May they complete the generation of goodness and awareness.
> May they clear away the two distortions and associated
>   conditioning.
> May we all attain the two pure forms.

INSTRUCTION:

Then express your wishes and prayers to all four kinds of guests and conclude the ritual with customary prayers of dedication, aspiration, and good fortune.

FROM THE RITUAL TEXT:

> Through the power that comes from this bountiful giving
> May we awaken naturally in order to help beings.
> May all beings who were not freed by earlier buddhas
> Be freed by giving.
>
> Any elemental demons who remain here,
> Wherever you are, under the ground, on the ground, or in
>   the sky,

Always be loving and kind to all beings
And engage the Dharma day and night.

Through this goodness, may all beings
Complete the generation of goodness and wisdom.
May they attain the two pure forms
That arise from goodness and wisdom.

Like a wish-fulfilling gem or a magic tree,
May I fulfill the hopes of all beings
Without the tensions of effort or strain.
May everyone have the good fortune for their dreams to
        come true.

◇◇◇

Rituals are dramas, a sequence of words, images, and actions that speak to parts of you that are not responsive to the conceptual mind. They remind you that life is rich and complex, that it cannot be understood or encompassed by the conceptual mind, and that as long as you live through thinking, there will be aspects of life that you ignore or dismiss. When you rest in mind nature while performing a ritual, not thinking about the words and meanings but just letting the imagery and the sentiments arise on their own, you may feel the various elements of the ritual calling to different parts of you, playing an intricate piece of music with your mind and body as instruments, and leaving you feeling cleansed, balanced, and at peace.

This is how magic works. It changes how you experience the world, both the world out there and the world within. When you do these rituals regularly over a period of time, the way you experience life gradually changes, moving you toward a mythic approach to life, not in a superstitious way, but one in which signs and symbols come alive and speak to you in their own language.

The power of ritual is not exclusive to Vajrayana. It is active in every tradition of Buddhism. Through rituals like this one, I learned to pay attention to aspects of life that I had previously ignored or been unaware of. The ritual of leaving a bit of food on my plate at the end of every meal and dedicating it to the hungry ghosts put me in touch with greed and miserliness. The ritual of taking refuge with my parents on each side of me and those with whom I have difficulty right in front of me taught me that I had to work out a relationship with every facet of life. Offering rituals of every conceivable description led me to enjoy the sights and sounds of the world without any sense of possession. Through the dark offerings to the protectors I came to see that reactive emotions have no ground and can become sources of understanding and insight when they are experienced as movements in mind.

In our culture we no longer honor the gods. Many practitioners of Western Buddhism dismiss this dimension of practice as superstitious and unnecessary. In doing so, they reinforce imbalances in their practice and imbalances in their lives. Those imbalances almost always take the form of ignoring — ignoring the body as I did, ignoring one or more patterns of reactivity, or ignoring whole aspects of life. It is better to address those imbalances while we still can, before they corrupt or destroy the good we do, before they do real damage to others, the world we live in, or ourselves, before they solidify as we age, before they kill us. The gods are there. Sooner or later they demand attention. We ignore them at our peril.

CHAPTER 8

Living Practice

It was my turn to lead the chants. I knew something was up—I could just tell. Suspicious, resentful, more than a little fearful, I watched my fellow retreatants enter the temple. Three people paused at the door to talk. Ah, I thought, it begins. What are they planning? How are they going to attack me? The conversation broke up, they made their bows and took their seats. Two other people were laughing as they came in. What were they laughing about? My coming embarrassment, discomfort, or pain?

Something shifted, and I dropped into a clear empty knowing. There was no plot. Nothing was going on. Nothing! And yet, at the same time I knew everyone had it in for me. I just knew it! I sat there for a few minutes quite stunned. The only turmoil in the room was the fear, paranoia, anger, and resentment in me. It was all there, vivid, visceral—and devoid of any substance or ground.

A short cough caught my attention. I looked around and saw that everyone was now seated, waiting quietly for me to begin. I started the chants, and the clouds of fear and anger drifted away leaving no trace or trail. Still, the stark contrast between raging emotion and empty knowing left an impression—a disturbing and pointed lesson in "Don't believe your feelings."

The world we experience consists of thoughts, feelings, and sensations. Everything else is a construction. I had had a difficult day, hours and hours of an unruly mind in an agitated body. I was tired, unhappy, and uncertain about my ability to keep going in the retreat. But the story I was caught in? It was a construction—thoughts, feelings, and sensations woven together. It was my construction. Mine! At the same time, the momentum of practice had dropped me into mind nature. The construction was nothing more than a story. There it was — a full-blown emotional reaction in clear empty knowing.

Movement in mind does not by itself cause you to fall into confusion and reaction. You fall into confusion and reaction because as soon as the mind moves, something in you takes the movement as I or other. That something has many names, but it is sufficient to say that it is a deeply conditioned pattern with a great deal of momentum. When it operates, the field of experience splits in two and you have once again taken birth in samsara.

A conceptual or cognitive understanding is of little help here. The conceptual mind is slow and weak. Nor is it a matter of observation, observing the contents of your mind. That just reinforces a sense of I separate from what you experience. Through practice, you discover the possibility of the world not splitting into two. As you train that way of experiencing, both in meditation and in life, that way of experiencing becomes part of you.

Meeting the Mystery

During the three-year retreat, a fellow retreatant asked Kalu Rinpoche to give the reading transmission for Karma Chakmé's autobiography. Karma Chakmé was a 17th century teacher in Tibet, a profound master whose practices and prayers we did regularly. As was custom, Rinpoche read the Tibetan text very quickly. I could follow only the general gist. But at one point, I heard what he was reading very clearly. "At this point in my practice, I did not know whether these experiences were the blessings of buddhas or the machinations of demons." He paused, and then read the sentence again, slowly and clearly. He paused again, and then read the same sentence a third time. Then he continued with the rest of the text, reading it so quickly that again I could barely follow the words.

Stuff happens in mystical practice, and it is not always clear what it is. If the experience is pleasant or blissful, we usually think, "That's good." If the experience is painful or frightening, we usually think,

"What am I doing wrong?" But it is hard to tell. Good experiences may seduce us into old patterns. Difficult experiences may wake us up and lead us to pay more attention. From a mystical perspective, which is bad and which is good?

Freedom in Reactivity

Suppose you are having a difficult time in your life and in your practice. Strange, inexplicable, and disturbing experiences arise unpredictably, sometimes as strong, powerful emotions, sometimes as physical pain, sometimes illusions or hallucinations.

You practice mindfulness, noting what happens in your body when you have these experiences and what stories run through your mind. This practice reduces your reactivity, but it doesn't really help. Basically, you don't want to experience those strange feelings. By making them objects of attention you are able to hold them at arm's length.

The strange experiences keep coming. You feel more and more out of balance. You practice taking and sending, taking in the struggles of others who have similar problems, and giving away your own well-being and joy in life. But that approach doesn't work either. Part of you does not care what others feel or experience. It just wants these problems to go away.

They don't. They continue. Perhaps they are the work of gods and demons? You propitiate these demons, you make offerings to them, you thank them for bringing you this kind of experience, and you assure them you have understood their message. Then you tell them, "Would you kindly leave me alone?" They don't listen. Perhaps they feel you are more interested in yourself than in them?

Pushed into a corner, you decide to be more decisive. You set up a protection circle, become your personal deity, and banish the disruptors from your environment, threatening them with death and destruction if they don't leave you alone. Even so, your physical pains, the reactive emotions, and the hallucinations continue.

All your efforts, whether mystical or magical, are about control. You are caught in the basic pattern of samsara, trying to control what you experience. The illusion of control is an indication of a lack of freedom. Freedom is the ability to be in whatever arises, without being consumed by it, without pushing it away.

You can analyze these experiences and reduce them to nothing, but that doesn't change anything. You can trace them to early childhood, or to past lives, but that doesn't change anything, either. You can consult your dreams and look for signs. You can even figure out exactly what kind of energy imbalance or demon is plaguing you, and apply the indicated remedies. But that doesn't change anything, either. You are still trying to control what you experience.

Eventually you have to face the fact that this is your life right now and there is nothing you can do about it. You go about your life, be in the pain, the frenzy, the craziness, and the hallucinations, and experience them as best you can. You fall into confusion and reaction, of course, but there is always a break, a moment of clarity, however short. The pain and hallucinations keep coming, but you keep coming back to that clarity. You do this a hundred times, maybe a thousand times, maybe ten or a hundred thousand times. You just keep doing it until you are able to be in the pain in your body, the craziness of your reactions, and the bewildering hallucinations that rage in your mind, and be clear, awake, and at peace at the same time.

This is one way of living practice.

Difficult Situations

Towards the end of my teacher's first visit to the West in 1973, I was sitting with him in his room at the new center in Vancouver. Out of the blue, he said, "Ken, what they say in the sutras is true."

There are hundreds of sutras. What on earth was he referring to? I had no idea. All I could do was ask, "What do they say in the sutras?"

"Old age is a drag."

Poignant and to the point—my teacher rarely wasted words. Over the years I have come back to this exchange again and again.

Life is life. It is what it is. We do not end suffering by trying to make life into something it is not. We end suffering when we stop struggling and be in life just as it is—in all its ups and downs, its rhythms and its messiness, its joys and pains. Life is unpredictable. Earthquakes, wildfires, hurricanes, and floods can change our lives in a moment, as can riots, wars, famines, and plagues. Inequity, malevolence, unfairness, and injustice exist in every society and every political system. Friends do become enemies and enemies do become friends. Death does await all of us, and it can come at any time. And old age is a drag.

A few times in my life I have been in very difficult situations, situations in which I could not see any way forward. In my practice sessions, I would, to the best of my ability, rest in the confusion that swirled inside me. I suppose it was the years of effort that made that resting possible, even though those efforts had often seemed paltry and ineffective.

Difficult situations are difficult because they involve conflict—externally, internally, or both. I rest in the conflict, and all the confusion it entails. I let the stories play themselves out. I let my feelings come and go. Bit by bit, everything calms down and grows quiet and dark, the quiet of a dark night with no moon or stars. As I rest in that darkness, a clarity sometimes arises, and with it a sense of direction. Who or what discerns that clarity and that direction I don't know.

The clarity does not illumine anything. It does not give me a better understanding. It just indicates a direction. Where that direction leads or what I will encounter I have no idea. There is a direction—nothing more.

Something in me seems to know that if I move in the direction indicated by the clarity, whatever happens, even if the situation becomes worse, it will be okay—that is, I can live with it.

When I then face the situation squarely, my instinct for self-preservation falls away, pain and difficulty are put into perspective, the shallowness of identity and self is revealed, and the illusion of what I think I need is shattered. Adversity can draw out a knowing that offers both freedom and peace, even when everything goes very, very badly.

This is also a way to live practice.

The Hammer

> "There's a big fat hammer up above, beyond the blue in the sky," he told me. "It's just up there waitin'. One day, when you least expect it, that hammer comes streakin' down on you like Big Pink's fist. That's the ultimate test for a boxer, for any man. It's the punch you don't see comin'. There's nothing you can do about it but try your best and recover. That's what you did against Mikey. You did good."

The quotation comes from *The Long Fall* by Walter Mosley. After that bout, Leonid McGill, the central character in the novel, gives up boxing despite the encouragement from Gordo, his trainer. McGill goes on to reflect:

> But what I hadn't understood at the time was that Gordo wasn't just talking about the ring. That hammer was waiting for everybody. It came at you in the form of cancer, infidelity, the tax man, or a comet out of the western sky here to annihilate any creature over fifty kilos in weight.

Mahler's Sixth Symphony. Thor's hammer. The blow you don't see coming. You cannot prevent it. You cannot protect yourself from it. It happens.

When that hammer comes down, your life changes. You become a different person. You learn things that you didn't know before, things that you may or may not have wanted to know—about life, about people, about society, and about yourself. There is nothing new here, but each of us has to uncover this truth for ourselves. We can read about it, we can study it, and we can work with it in meditation or prayer. But when the hammer comes down, we have to live it — and that is different.

The hammer has taught me that any anger I feel about it means that I am living in the past. Revenge, retribution are chains that bind me to what happened. Anger, sorrow, bitterness, grief — all these feelings are in the way. They are how my system mobilizes itself to meet the situation or to recover from the shock. But when the anger and sorrow linger, when I build a life around them — a life defined by bitterness or hate, a life around never letting go, never moving on — it is because something in me wants to go back to how the world was before the hammer came down. That part of me is living in the past.

I cannot wish away the lingering anger or bitterness. Such feelings can rarely be excised by an act of will. My world has forever changed, and mind and body have to adjust. It doesn't matter how awake or present I may be, I still experience loss and grief and all the physical and emotional reactions that accompany them. If anything, I experience them more vividly because I am not putting up a wall or trying to control what I experience. I am in it to the best of my ability, with no other agenda.

No agenda, I have found, is the key. When I stop trying to make anything happen, completely and utterly stop, a point comes where I am not there anymore. There is only experience. It is vivid, vivid beyond comprehension. And it is empty, groundless, whatever word you want to use. Form and emptiness. In that crucible of searing emotion and groundlessness, a different kind of knowing reveals itself. Without thinking or strategizing, I know what needs to be done, and I do it. I know what needs to be said, and I say it. It seems so natural that it feels like nothing, like I'm not doing anything at all.

This is also a way to live practice.

Living a Path

To live this way requires some form of awakening, some taste of freedom from the prison of self, the blindness of confusion, and the tyranny of emotional reactions. For a long time I sought the kind of awakening experiences that I had read about in books or heard about from others, but I have come to appreciate that awakening is like a diamond. The light of empty clarity is reflected, refracted, and diffracted in countless ways.

As I worked with students, I came to see that the details of the experience of awakening were less important than the shift that took place in the student. Did their experience fundamentally change how they experienced the world? Did it change how they lived their lives? I'm not talking about becoming a recluse or a monastic, though that is a choice some people make. The changes I looked for are about being more precise in how you move, how you speak, and how you conduct yourself moment to moment each day.

Most people find that a certain simplification is called for, a simplification that creates space in their lives to avoid being constantly reactive or disturbed. That simplification takes place at every level of their being, from how they walk and stand, how they speak, how they work and interact with others, to what they deem worthwhile and meaningful in their lives. Tokmé Zongpo in *The 37 Practices of a Bodhisattva* and Longchenpa in *30 Pieces of Sincere Advice*, pieces that both authors originally wrote for themselves, speak to these changes.

Once you have a clear understanding of what is possible, once you have learned how to develop the skills and capabilities you need, and once you have learned how to recognize and meet your internal material, then you can make use of your training to meet the questions and the yearnings you hold in your heart. In doing so, you set out on a path. I say *a path* rather than *the path* because there are many paths—84,000 according to tradition. And I say *a path* rather than *your path* because there is no sense of specialness or ownership here, no sense of fate or destiny. You travel a path, but the path you travel does not belong to you, nor to anyone else. It is simply the path you travel.

Once you have experienced some kind of awakening, the tenor of practice changes. The metaphor of a flower unfolding becomes just as important as the metaphor of traveling a path. The key to unfolding is to rest deeply inside and let movements — whether sensory, thought, or feeling — arise and resolve themselves. Your ability to do this will depend on your skill and capacity. Take the time and make the effort to build the skills and capacity you will need. In the Tibetan tradition, this is the path of method. Letting empty clear knowing unfold is the path of release. Do both, alternating them from one session of formal practice to another or from one day to another.

Mastery

In the Mahamudra tradition, the fourth and final level is called *no practice*. The terminology belies what is going on. The level of no practice evolves out of a mastery of skills and their deep assimilation from applying them in many different situations. When you watch an expert horse-rider, a virtuoso violinist, or a skilled woodworker, it seems there is no effort involved, but the ease and precision with which they move testify to the years of effort they have practiced their respective disciplines. Doing nothing in meditation means that you have trained both the ability to rest in mind nature and the skills to meet what arises in experience — so deeply that they take place on their own without apparent effort. Doing nothing in life means that you do what you do as if it were nothing at all, because knowing and acting are not separate — like the rider, the violinist, or the woodworker.

Mastery develops through practice, and there is no end to practice. We say that a good rider is one with his or her horse. That apparent unity comes about through practice. It is the same with the empty clear knowing of mind nature. You rest in it in formal meditation sessions. You touch it in your daily life. There is no end to resting in it.

There is no end to touching it. You do not even think about how to apply it to your life, for the moment such a thought arises, you have already separated from your life and from the clear empty knowing.

To live practice is to empty experience of self — constantly. In this way you keep moving into a knowing in which awareness and experience are not separated.

Living practice begins only when you have mastered one or more practices. What does it take to master a practice? Regardless of the discipline, there are three steps. Learn the method. Practice it until it becomes second nature. Remove everything in you that prevents it from operating when it is called for. Living practice is not a matter of remembering. If you have to remember, you are already lost. As Chekawa Yeshe Dorje wrote in *Mind Training in Seven Points*, "Mastery means it happens even when you are distracted."

There are thousands of practices in Vajrayana. If you are reading this, you have probably been exposed to more than you can ever master in one lifetime. As my own teacher advised, pick a few practices that speak to you and master them. Each practice has to become so much a part of you that it operates on its own.

Here are the practices that spoke to me.

Stable attention

Stable attention is essential. Without it you have nothing. Attention has two qualities, mindfulness and awareness. Mindfulness is knowing what you are doing. Awareness is being aware of what is going on.

Carry a teaspoon of water through a crowded room. Attention to holding the spoon without spilling the water is mindfulness. Attention to where everyone is to avoid being bumped is awareness. Cultivate these two qualities in everything you do, including meditation.

Don't confuse result with method. Take right speech, for instance. It is described as true, relevant, kind, and calm. If you try to speak that way, you end up tongue-tied. Instead, listen to the sound of your own voice as if you are listening to another person. The two qualities of attention are immediately there: you know what you are saying and you are aware of how it sounds. This is method. Right speech is result, or will be after a bit of practice.

In the same vein, doing something slowly is method, not result. Ask a street fighter. They make a move slowly in order to make it correctly. They stop at any point in the move in order not to be out of balance. They train on unstable surfaces in order not to be out of balance anywhere. But that's not how they fight. When they fight, they move quickly, smoothly, and fluidly. The result is not slow movement. It's staying alive.

Train attention until you can do everything you do during the day in attention. A sign of training is that a chipped dish, a missed turn, or an unintended edge in your voice tells you that you have fallen out of attention, regardless of how or why it happened.

Death and impermanence

Death is a mystery. Make it your friend. It is part of life in the same way that birth is part of life. One is the beginning. One is the end.

To be in the mystery, don't do anything with what arises. When you react to what arises, when you suppress it or spin stories about it, you are doing something with it.

To enter the mystery, hold these two together: you are going to die and you do not know when. What happens? Ordinary thinking, ordinary experiencing stops. Concerns about happiness, wealth, recognition, and respect lose their hold. Take this to heart.

Know that even spiritual yearnings — immortality, eternal bliss, universal selfhood, or transcendent purity — are daydreams, enticements that distract you from the mystery of death. So, too, are all theories and beliefs asserting that there is nothing beyond this life.

Through all the ups and downs of life — success and failure, gain and loss, the joy of family, children, and friends, the loneliness of rejection or isolation — remember: this, too, shall pass. That simple phrase always has the power to shift how you experience life.

Make death your constant companion. Make it a secret practice, unbeknownst to others. Feel death's breath on the back of your neck in everything you do, driving to work, taking a walk, playing with your children. Live each moment as if it were your last.

Live in the totality of your life. Past, present, and future, they are all present in each moment. In that field, moment by moment know where the imbalance is and know the direction of balance. That is the direction of the present. That is what needs to done.

Do what needs to be done without any expectation that you will see or know the result of your efforts.

Bodhicitta, the Bodhisattva Vow, and Mahayana Mind Training

Vajrayana is based on the bodhisattva vow, on compassion and emptiness. Whenever you have the opportunity to take the bodhisattva vow in a formal ceremony, do so. It makes a difference.

The essence of the bodhisattva vow is to step out of your own confusion. Learn to go empty whenever a reaction arises. As a way to start, train to take a breath before you say anything, even in casual conversations. With practice, you will develop the ability to go empty before you speak. Then touch the clear empty knowing that is the union of compassion and emptiness, and speak from there.

Cultivate compassion until you have no skin. Cultivate compassion until the pain of others is a knife in your heart. Cultivate the ability to be in that intense pain and be clear and at peace at the same time — compassion and emptiness.

Be courteous, treat others with humanity and justice, and celebrate their successes and achievements. These are the social expressions of the four immeasurables.

When you are in pain, emotional or physical, don't try to make it go away. Instead, use taking and sending as a way to be in the pain and not struggle with it. When everything is going well in your life and you are happy and carefree, don't try to hold on to it. Again, use taking and sending as a way to be in your life and not be taken over by your good fortune.

When other people are having difficulty, be with them in their pain. Don't try to make them feel better. When you are with them in their pain without struggling, they may find a way to be in their pain, too.

When someone acts in a way that is incomprehensible and inexplicable, ask yourself, "Where would I have to be to act that way?" This is not a matter of analysis or deduction. It is a matter of direct knowing. If you can't answer that question, do taking and sending until you know their struggles in yourself. Do the same when someone does something extraordinarily kind, brilliant, or creative. Where would you have to be to be able to do that?

Devotion and prayer

Your relationship with your teachers has a mythic dimension. Respect it. Your teacher is how you experience awakened mind, buddha.

Devotion and prayer are ways to form a relationship with your teacher that even death cannot touch.

Develop devotion through prayer, through reaching out to what you do not know. When you pray, reach out to what you yearn to know, whether in the form of your teacher, a past master, your personal deity, or your protector. To whomever you pray, pray to them as the embodiment of awakened mind, as the actual knowing of mind nature.

When you pray, feel that your teacher or diety is present in front of you, above your head, or in your heart. While it is said that the first develops virtue, the second energy, and the third insight, choose whichever gives you the strongest sense of connection.

Say prayers such as *Devotion Pierces My Heart*, prayers in which you acknowledge all the ways your efforts fall short. Pray to your teacher or teachers to find the energy to take practice further.

Make your chosen focus of devotion a constant companion. Find one or two short prayers that really speak to you and make them part of you. Find a prayer, memorize it, and repeat it continuously when you are walking, working out, cooking, or gardening.

Through teacher-union practice, you come to experience your mind as your teacher's mind: you come to know mind nature. As practice matures, mind nature shows you what to do. This is not a conceptual knowing. It is a knowing you uncover through devotion and prayer.

Deity practice

Rest in the experience of things without seeing them as things. If labels come to mind, let them come and go as you would any other thought. In this way, the world arises as experience, but it is not your experience.

Don't try to see others as the deity and the world as the deity's pure land. A conceptual approach will leave you in confusion.

To hear sound as mantra, listen to the silence in sound. Silence is always there. You just forget it when you hear a noise or someone speaks to you. To enter the mystery of sound, listen to silence and sound at the same time.

To know thoughts and feelings as the play of awareness, don't try to transform emotional reactions into timeless awareness or anything else. Instead, when thoughts and emotional reactions arise, touch clear empty knowing. Sometimes that's all that is necessary. Sometimes you have to stay in the turmoil until you discover peace and clarity in the reaction itself.

Magical apparition

Practice mindfulness, death and impermanence, compassion, and deity as if you are dreaming.

Faith is one way to raise energy. There are others, such as body scanning, loving kindness practice, mantra recitation, energy circulation, and so on. Cultivate the method that works for you until it operates on its own.

Keep a short prayer going in your heart, a prayer that expresses your deepest spiritual yearnings.

Whenever you find yourself thinking, come back to the prayer.

When shifts in awareness arise on their own, don't hold on to them. Rest in them.

Experience grows into knowing in the same way that a sapling grows into a tree. You don't make a tree grow. It grows when you nourish it with care and attention.

Open to everything you experience and look at what is aware. Something shifts. Rest in that shift as you go about your life.

Protector

Train to sense balance and imbalance in your life — without recourse to the conceptual mind. Train the same way that you sense balance and imbalance when you ride a bicycle — your body knows and acts before you do.

Move in the direction of balance, changing direction moment to moment as the point of balance shifts. Don't think about this. When you have trained deeply enough, it happens — again, like riding a bicycle.

Train to meet any and every difficulty in your life with the four stages of conflict in order:

First, resolve the issue calmly, using the resources at hand.

Failing that, resolve it expansively, bringing in additional resources.

Failing that, align with the situation, and let the situation compel a resolution.

Failing that, bring an end to the situation in which the conflict arises.

If you can, walk away. If not, submit to what is called for.

Do it without anger, bitterness, or desire for revenge, for these always leave a mark.

Take whatever happens in your life as something that has been given to you.

In the case of good fortune, give thanks and use the good fortune to deepen your practice. Don't let it lull you to sleep.

In the case of misfortune, give thanks and use the misfortune to deepen your practice. This is usually not easy and may take time.

Direct awareness

Return to what is already there and rest. What is already there? At first, it's the breath, then it's experience, then it's clear empty knowing, and then it cannot be put into words.

In direct awareness, all the other practices come into play. Mastery is essential.

Stable attention. Rest. Whenever you notice you have fallen into distraction, come back to what is already there and rest.

Death and impermanence. Don't name experience. A name ties you to the past.

Taking and sending. Don't try to control what you experience. Don't try to make it any different from what it is. Good or bad, be in it.

Faith and devotion. Go deep into the mystery. What you are cannot be named or explained. Trust it.

Creation phase. Be what recognizes what is arising. That is the deity.

Completion phase. Let go of being anything. Rest in what is already there.

Magical apparition. Thoughts, feelings, sensations arise like reflections in a mirror, mists in the morning sun, rainbows in the sky.

Protector. Feel the imbalance. Sense the direction of balance. Move in that direction.

As you go about your day, look right at what you are experiencing, whether it is a thought, feeling, or sensation. Look at it as if you were looking at a reflection in a mirror. There is usually a slight shift — words drop away into a clear, quiet, indescribable knowing.

Now look at that knowing. You see nothing. Go empty. Let experience arise and be empty at the same time. As experience and awareness mix, a deeper knowing dawns, a knowing in which experience and awareness are not separate.

Additional points

Return to what is already there and rest. Nothing more is needed. Do it again, and again, and again.

At first do this for short periods, taking a break when you run out of juice. As your ability grows, extend and include. Extend to longer periods of time. Include more and more of your experience.

Keep mind and body supple and flexible. You are growing a tree, not building a machine. If you train too much, too hard, or too quickly, your mind and your whole being end up bruised, battered, and stiff. This is not helpful.

Even in short moments of resting, awareness may stir up your internal material. Do balancing practices regularly — such as physical movement, tai chi, qi gong, or yoga, as well as ritual offerings, asking the protectors for help, and making peace with gods and demons.

Conclusion

Samsara, the cycle of existence, is not the world in which we live, but the way we live in the world we experience. We struggle with what arises in experience, and that struggle is characterized by reaction and confusion. Because of the difficulties I experienced, I could not rely on a traditional path of practice. I had to find another way to respond to the small internal voice that called to me. In this vein, I took heart in the words of the 16th century historian Pawo Tsulak Trengwa:

Although I haven't visited frightening charnel grounds,
I haven't faced anything more frightening than
Beliefs based on the poisonous five reactive emotions
And the eight concerns of conventional success.

To these, I applied practice the way rock meets bone.
The eight concerns dissolved like rainbows,
Poisonous reactive emotions became my friends, and
Thinking attached to emotional reactions released itself.

One day in 2008 in New Mexico, the second verse came to life in a way that was indeed like magic. Since then, an unfathomable peace that I cannot put into words has permeated every facet of my life. Now and then I forget it, but when I return, it greets me with a quiet joy.

We do not choose a path. We can only take the one that forms at our feet.

Postscript

Mahayana and Vajrayana cannot be separated. Vajrayana is a branch of Mahayana and Mahayana practice is woven into Vajrayana practice. This interweaving goes back to the beginnings of Vajrayana and it can be seen clearly in the figure of Niguma, the late medieval Indian mystic on whose teachings a good part of this book is based. She was a mahasiddha, a profound mystic and master of the deity and high-level energy transformation practices for which Vajrayana is known. It was precisely through these practices that she sought to realize the bodhisattva ideal. Drawing on themes expressed in the *Flower Garland Sutra* and other Mahayana sutras, the aspirations she expresses in this prayer stir the heart with their breath-taking reach and awe-inspiring vision.

Niguma's Mystical Wishes:
The King of Spiritual Intentions

I pay homage to all buddhas and bodhisattvas.

Through the wonderful workings of compassion
Of myriad buddhas throughout time and space
May each and every one of these wishes
Be fulfilled in keeping with my prayers.

From this moment on, in every possible way,
May I please my teachers with immeasurable devotion,
Give them without limit the purest in body, speech, and comfort,
And not take even a moment's break in making their work blossom.

In every life, whenever I study, teach, meditate, or practice,
May I not encounter bad professors, bad teachers,
Bad companions, or bad patrons.
May I study with the finest gurus and find awakening
      through them.

In all my births, may I have good parentage and good health,
A pleasing voice, a fine body, charisma, and power,
And, naturally endowed with longevity, followers, wealth, and
      spiritual qualities,
Be respected by all.

In every life wherever I am born
May I create no strife but be gracious to all —
Every being whenever they see, hear, touch, or think of me,
Never tiring of my charming and genial mien.

For beings as numerous as the sky is vast,
May I not only be a protector, a source of hope, and a champion,
But fulfill their every hope and desire
Exactly as they themselves wish.

May those friends who wish to help me
And practice the same aspirations in thought, word, and deed
From now on always be close to me
And flourish in the joy of pure experience.

However I take birth, may I be a wishing gem
And bring happiness to all beings
By fulfilling their wants and needs as soon as they think of them
And showering them with infinite riches.

May all beings in every place I live
Be free from illness, madness, strife, and hardship,

Live long, be well, and have comfort and spiritual qualities,
Flourishing in goodness and good fortune.

In this life, in all my lives,
Through my mastering the wealth of the Treasury of Heaven,
And sending the four kinds of gifts in every direction,
May all beings, through the ten perfections, ripen and be free.

Through the highest and fullest knowing, free from reaction
        and restriction,
Of every possible experience in samsara and nirvana
May every possible sphere of understanding throughout time
Become clear in a single instant.

Through my wearing the three disciplines with grace and
        without flaw
And being unrivalled in honor and praise from heaven and earth,
May all beings take up the highest of ethics
And perfect every possible good quality.

Content in a mountain retreat, with food and clothes,
With not a moment's disturbance from inside or out,
May my complete understanding and endless efforts
Ripen and free each and every being.

May powerful gods and demons, the arrogant ones, all of them,
Without even a moment's conjuring or command on my part
Offer their lives and hearts, obey me as servants,
And with their powerful magic protect the teachings.

Through my genuine love and compassion,
May all beings throughout the three realms
Allay the harmful hostility they harbor for others
And rest like a child in a mother's love.

When the time comes for me to die,
May I not be in agony. As what is true becomes clear
And what takes form arises naturally to help others,
May my remains and relics inspire beings.

In every possible buddha realm
May I present offerings for oceans of eons
To oceans of buddhas as numerous as atoms in the universe
With the sky-like vastness of Ever-present Good's cloud
        of offerings.

As oceans of buddha realms become utterly clear,
Through pure action and limitless understanding,
May I see whole oceans of experience
And know directly oceans of timeless awareness.

As the melodious speech of oceans of buddhas becomes
        utterly clear,
May I give voice in Brahma's cadence to the reaches of space,
Teach the Dharma to beings in their own languages,
And lead every being to buddhahood.

Just as in the magical accounts of Ever-present Good,
May the magic of absorption without limit become utterly clear,
And every possible buddha and buddha realm
Instantly appear on a single atom.

Like the depth and breadth of the realms of beings and the oceans,
The end of the sky and the infinity of the totality of experience,
May my wishes, absorptions, and actions
Be impossible to measure—truly limitless in their depth and scope.

May I take form as countless universal monarchs,
Fulfill the hopes of beings and protect spiritual countries,

Govern buddha realms extending through the vastness of space,
And bring peace to every being.

In the future, when the age of plagues and wars
Brings struggle and ruin to beings,
May I become a monarch of medicine
And instantly calm their struggles and pain.

When the age of famine brings hunger and thirst,
May food and drink, silk, silver, gold, and wealth,
All that is wonderful, gather in clouds filling the sky
And shower sensory pleasures everywhere.

Until the oceans of samsara have been emptied,
May great waves of awakening action
Teach to every being whose numbers fill all space,
Exactly what will help each of them.

All beings who have taken a wrong way, the powerful, the arrogant,
Those who could not be taught by buddhas throughout all space
        and time,
May I teach each and every one of them
And lead them in an instant to buddhahood.

As long as any sentient being remains in samsara,
May spontaneous effortless actions
That ripen and free beings without exception,
Arise naturally and continuously for the welfare of beings.

Oceans of buddhas throughout time and space
When they were ordinary beings or bodhisattvas
For countless eons gave rise to awakening mind, prayed,
Completed goodness and awareness, and became buddhas.

Endowed with such excellence and with oceans of talent
They worked to ripen and free countless beings.
When all their wishes and efforts are combined together,
May my wish and my effort be even greater.

Because the welfare of others arises naturally and without limit,
For all who give rise to faith and delight in supreme awakening
And make these wishes themselves, may these my wishes,
All of them, every one of them, come to complete fruition.

May all the wonderful richness of good fortune and well-being
Throughout all time and space, in samsara and nirvana,
Flow continuously like a great river
And infuse everyone, myself and others, everywhere.

The King of Spiritual Intentions ends here.

In response to the heartfelt requests of Ann Craig and Claudia Hansson, I,
Ken McLeod, building on the careful work of Sarah Harding, translated this
prayer in Windsor, California, in July, 2021. May it ignite the fire of awakening in
all who take it to heart.

The Magic of Faith

In the sky in front of me is my teacher, appearing as Niguma.
Every part of me, physical, emotional, mental, and spiritual, prays
to her to be free from samsara's struggles:

I and all beings, infinite in number,
    take refuge in Buddha, Dharma, and Sangha.
I and all beings, infinite in number,
    take refuge in the teacher, in practice, and in what arises
    in experience.
I and all beings, infinite in number,
    take refuge in experience, empty, vivid, immediate.

Repeat three times.

Beings are numberless: I vow to free them all.
Reactions are endless: I vow to release them all.
Doors to experience are infinite: I vow to enter them all.
Ways of awakening are limitless: I vow to know them all.

Repeat three times.

Here in this forest, in the middle of my life,
Trees close in: a darkening path awaits my feet.
Much have I learned, yet more I seek to know.
What sense does it make for me to turn back now?

Buddhas and bodhisattvas,
Wherever you may be,
Please help me to find a way.

Repeat many times.

Though teachers assure me time and again
About what they feel I know and understand,
My heart still longs for what no words will serve.
What is there to do but trust this yearning and go on?

Buddhas and bodhisattvas,
Wherever you may be,
Please help me to find a way.

Repeat many times.

"Find Niguma," I'm told. With the magic of that name
I find a strength that gently leads me on.
Dark the way, yet clear my heart and mind.
How does this mystery show me where to go?

Buddhas and bodhisattvas,
Wherever you may be,
Please help me to find a way.

Repeat many times.

The skeletons of my life are scattered all about.
So is the rotting flesh of love and hate and fear,
And hair, the wild, wild hair of thought, wafts everywhere:
Oh, Sosa Grove, what have you brought me to?

Buddhas and bodhisattvas,
Wherever you may be,
Please help me to find a way.

Repeat many times.

"What are you doing here?" a voice shouts from the sky,
"This place isn't safe, especially for the likes of you.
Begone, before my companions soon arrive,
And feast on you, your flesh, and, yes, your bones."

Niguma!

Dark tan your skin, black your hair, and
Three eyes blazing like fire.
The rattle of a drum in your right hand
Summons your companions, intent and fierce.
Your left holds a skull cup, and encircles Shiva's staff.
At ease you sit as you turn your gaze on me.

"Here, take this gold," I plead, "the last of all the wealth I've known."
"Is that all you have?" she sneers, tossing it all away.
Grinning, her cannibal companions lick their lips with glee.
For me what's left now? What more can I do?

Use either of these two prayers to pray with the deep devotion that comes when all
hope is gone and you have nothing left to lose:

Treasured teacher,
In your presence I awaken free from time.
I pray to you.
For the sake of all beings,
Give me energy to let belief in self fall away.
Give me energy to see through life's illusions.
Give me energy to master enchantment and dream.
Give me energy to know the sheer clarity of being itself.

   Or

Treasured teacher, I pray to you.
Give me energy to let belief in self fall away.
Give me energy to see through life's illusions.
Give me energy to let reactive thinking end.
Give me energy to know mind has no beginning.
Give me energy to let confusion resolve itself.
Give me energy to know that life is empty presence.

She smiles and, as I feel her light touch,
I slowly rise into the sky.
When I look into her deep black eyes,
I meet space—open, vast, beyond all measure.

"Like and dislike are the mind's disease,
Certain to drown you in samsara's seas.
Know that there is nothing here at all,
And then, my child, everything is gold.

Experience arises like magic.
If you practice like magic
You awaken like magic
Through the power of faith.

Don't think about your teacher or your practice.
Don't think about what is real or not real.
Don't think about anything at all.
Don't control what you experience.
Just rest in how you are right now."

With these words, she dissolves into light,
And, like water pouring into water,
She and I become one.

Rest without reference and then conclude with this dedication.

I let go of all the good that comes from this practice:
May it touch everyone and everything I know.
May it ease the pain of struggle everywhere.
And awaken new possibilities for all.

At the request of Lawrence Ladden of Pennsylvania, who wanted a way to connect with Niguma and her teaching, Ken McLeod composed this short practice in the month of November, 2008 in Los Angeles, California. Some years later, Dan Jorgensen requested a few changes in the text.

NOTES

1. The practice is loosely based on Khyungpo's first meeting with Niguma.
2. Sosa Grove is the name of the charnel ground where Khyungpo Naljor was told to look for Niguma.

Mastery of the Deathless
A Simple Daily Practice for Lady Wishing Wheel

om svasti siddhim
I bow respectfully to the noble immortal one;
Whenever we think of her, she vanquishes the threats of the four
      obsessions.
In order that we may attain longevity and other ordinary
      capabilities as well as supreme awakening
I set forth this, her daily practice ritual.

At dawn or in the early part of the day, place yourself comfortably on your
meditation mat in the posture of meditation.

REFUGE AND AWAKENING MIND

I take refuge in my teacher, union of the Three Jewels.
In order to help others, I practice being the goddess
      Wishing Wheel.

Repeat this three times.

GENERATION OF GOODNESS (OPTIONAL)

I am Tara. Light shines from my heart
And invites her and her heirs to appear before me.

vajra samaja

I go for refuge to the Three Jewels.
I acknowledge each and every unwholesome act.
I rejoice in the virtue of all beings.
I hold to the awakening of buddhas.

Until I awaken I take refuge
In the Buddha, the Dharma, and the Noble Assembly.
In order to take full care of others and myself
I form the mind of awakening.
In forming this intention for true awakening
I welcome all beings as my guests.
By immersing myself in the joyful activity of awakening,
May I awaken fully and help all beings.

Repeat this prayer, let the gathering dissolve, and then rest without reference.

May all beings be happy, be free from struggle,
Never want for joy, and rest in great equanimity.

CREATION PHASE

om shunyata jñana vajra svabhava atma koñ ham

From the sound of *hūm*, the energy of emptiness,
A protective enclosure of vajras appears.
Inside arises a palace of crystal
With a full moon throne on a white lotus flower.

The syllable *tam* appears and becomes
A white lotus flower bearing a *tam*.
Light shines from the flower and fulfills the two aims.
The light returns and the flower transforms:
Now I am Tara, white as the moon.

My smile is charming and peaceful.
Lights of five colors shine from my body.
My forehead, face, hands, and feet are graced by
The seven eyes of timeless awareness.

My right hand gestures in peerless giving;
My left holds with ring finger and thumb
A white lotus flower close to my heart.

I wear a white blouse, a five-color skirt,
And elegant jewelry set with pearls and stones.
My black hair is bound up with locks hanging freely.
I sit in vajra posture with a moon at my back.

My three points are marked by *om, ah*, and *hūm*.
Light from them invites the awareness-being: *vajra samaja.*
ja hūm bam ho: she and I are one.

Again I send out light and invite the buddhas of the five families:
"Empowering Deities, bestow empowerment on me."
To this request, the deities respond:
om sarva tathagata ahbhishekata samaya shriye hūm.

With these words they confer empowerment.
My body is filled with elixir and all impurities are washed away.
The head of the family, Amitabha, crowns me.
I send out deities who honor and praise me.

*om arya tara vajra argham padyam pukpé dhupé aloké gendhé névidya
    shapda praticha ah hūm svaha*

We gods and titans pay homage
By laying our crowns at your feet.
You, who save us from all catastrophes,
Mother savior, we honor and praise you.

MANTRA RECITATION

In my heart there is a lotus, moon, and wheel.
Above the center of the wheel is the syllable *tam*.
Above and below are the syllables *om* and *ha*,
The other eight syllables one above each spoke
Positioned clockwise, the color of the fall moon, clear and still.

Say the root mantra as the principal recitation:

om taré tuttaré turé svaha

To add the life extension:

Around the *tam* and between the *om* and *ha* sits the extension spell.
It radiates light which for both others and myself
Clears away confusion, enriches life and well-being,
Renders offerings to the noble ones and gathers energy from them,
And life essence from all that stand or move.
As it all soaks into me, I receive fullness of life and
      timeless wisdom.

om taré tuttaré turé mama aryu punyé jñana puktrim kuru svaha
(Give me life, goodness, awareness, and wealth)

Recite this mantra to build life power and for daily practice.

From time to time:

I ask my guru, the head of this family, to empower me with
      the deathless.
Moved by my devotion he sends light from his heart and
Gathers the vitality and essence of life from all that is and all
      that arises.
The vitality and essence are drawn in and fill his alms bowl.
It overflows, filling me with the elixir of the deathless.

Recite this spell as all this happens:

om taré tuttaré turé mama aryu punyé jñana puktrim kuru svaha

DISSOLUTION AND ARISING TO END THE PRACTICE PERIOD

The world and its inhabitants melt into light.
I, too, and the syllable *tam* melt
Into a sheer clarity free from reference.

Again I am White Tara, marked by the three syllables.
All experience is the play of deity, mantra, and timeless awareness.

DEDICATION, ASPIRATION, AND GOOD FORTUNE

Through this good may I and all beings
Quickly become the mother of all buddhas, the perfection
     of wisdom.
May the noble Tara look after us in all our lives.
May the good fortune of life, energy, and timeless awareness fill
     the whole universe.

TORMA (OFFERING CAKE) RITUAL

ram yam kam

In a bejeweled bowl the three syllables melt into light
To become an ocean of the purest elixir to be offered.

om ah hūm

Repeat three times.

Light from my heart invites the noble one
And her offspring into the space in front of me.

vajra samaja

padma kamalaya stvam

om tare tuttare saparivara idam balingta ka ka kahi kahi
Present the offering by repeating this three times.

Present the usual offerings with:

*om arya tara vajra argham padyam pukpé dhupé aloké ghendé névidya
    shabda praticha ah hūm svaha*
And praise with:

Mother Tara, who frees beings from the cycle of existence,
Fast-acting Tara, who frees beings from the eight threats,
Tara, who frees beings from illness,
This savior, I honor and praise.

Noble mother with your offspring,
Accept this offering and to me and those around me
Grant your protection and energy.
Give us full ability in sacred activity and length of life
And all ordinary and special attainments.

Recite the hundred-syllable mantra to acknowledge and remedy lapses.

Imagine that the guests dissolve into your heart.

DEDICATION, ASPIRATION, AND GOOD FORTUNE

Through this good may I and all beings
Quickly become the mother of all buddhas, the perfection
    of wisdom.
May the noble Tara look after us in all our lives.
May the good fortune of life, energy, and timeless awareness fill
    the whole universe.

Mother of the supreme buddha Amitabha,
Reliable giver of immortality,
Blessed one, holder of knowledge,
May the good fortune of Tara prevail.

Great Goddess, your blessings come the fastest
To enhance and strengthen life energy.
May all who connect with you through
This practice text in the lineage of Atisha
Attain your supreme powers.

In response to the request and offerings of Padme Tse-wang Palmo, a lady of noble birth, I, Lodrö Thaye, composed this daily practice for White Tara.

In response to requests from several students, I, Ken McLeod, translated this text in Los Angeles, California. May good come of these efforts.

A Concise Essential Offering Ritual for the Six-Armed Lord

Om svasti
I bow to teacher and lord, indivisible.

TORMA BLESSING

Charge the inner offerings and tormas as in deity practice.

om vajra amrita kundali hana hana hūm pāt
om svabhava shuddha sarva dharma svabhava shuddho ham

In empty presence, the syllable *yam* appears and turns into wind and *ram* into fire. Above them, *ah* becomes a skull cup filled with the five meats and five liquids and the syllables *hūm, bhrum, ām, dzring,* and *kham*. Winds blow, fires blaze, and the ten substances along with the syllables melt together. I draw and mix in the elixir of awareness from the hearts of all buddhas, creating a great sea of liquid timeless awareness.

om ah hūm ha ho hri
Repeat three times

om svabhava shuddha sarva dharma svabhava shuddho ham

In empty presence, in front of me, on a lotus and sun, *hūm* appears and turns into the Six-Armed Lord of Timeless Awareness, his body blue-black in color. His first pair of hands hold a chopper and skull cup, the second pair a rosary of human heads and a trident, and the last a hand-drum and noose. He wears a tiger-skin skirt, bone and snake jewelry, a necklace of severed heads, and sets of bells on his arms and legs. His two legs support him in the balanced posture and crush Obstacle-Maker. He has three eyes and bared fangs. His beard, eyebrows, and hair flare upwards. He is crowned by Buddha Unshakeable and bears a drop of cinnabar on his forehead. He stands, his back against the trunk of a sandalwood tree, in the middle of a blazing mass of fire.

On his left, from *bhyo* arises Shri Devi, black, riding a mule and holding a demon stick and a bag of pestilence. In front is Malefactor Kshetrapala, dark brown, holding a chopper and skull cup, riding a rabid black bear. On the right is Jinamitra, reddish black, holding a hand-drum and wheel. Behind is Takkiraja, black, holding a razor and skull cup filled with blood. On the left is Demon Lord Trakshé, holding a battle standard and skull cup containing a human heart, riding a black demon horse with white fetlocks, and wearing a flowing silk cape and felt boots.

Around them throng the seventy-five glorious lords and a sea of oath-bound protectors.

My heart radiates light that draws, from the sandalwood tree with a single trunk in the Cool Grove in the south-east, the Six-Armed Lord of Timeless Awareness, with the root and lineage gurus above, grimacing warriors on the right, smiling amazons on the left, and a horde consisting of oceans of committed protectors, local guardians, messengers, and those bound by oaths.

om vajra mahakala sapari wari kching
kching kching kching kching
kching kching kching kching
kching kching kching kching
kching kching kching kching
kching kching kching kching
vajra samaja ja hūm bam ho

hūm

This outer offering of fine heavenly things
That arise through interdependence
I present to the Lord and his retinue.
Please accept them for protecting the teachings.

*om shri mahakala sapari wari argham padyam pukpé dhupé aloké gendhé
    névidya shapda praticha hūm svaha*

om ah hūm

Although you do not move from the realm of totality
You take a wrathful form to subdue evil.
You who destroy the enemies of the teachings,
Great Black One, I bow to you.

ENGAGING OBLIGATION

Obligation gifts as vast as the offering clouds of Ever-present Good appear.

om vajra spharana kham

hūm
Fast-acting compassion, All Seeing One,
Great Black One with six arms,
Lord of energy and your retinue,
I'm here to engage your terrifying obligations.

All the riches of the world and everything in it
Arise naturally as clouds of wonderful offerings.
Treasures from fearful charnel grounds
Where evil forces were destroyed are spread all around.

The power of this contemplative's devotion magnifies
The commitment offerings enjoyed in the great mysteries.

With these offerings,
I sate your incomprehensible desires —

Ravens that soar like garudas,
Fleet horses and majestic yaks,
Graceful sheep and fierce dogs,
The thirteen-fold black offerings bedecked with ribbons
      and jewels,

Magic arrows adorned with silks and mirrors,
Knifed hearts packed with soul stones and spells,
Seas of medicine-juice and blood,
Mountains of sacrificial and power offerings,

And especially, mind itself, utter simplicity,
Single-minded faith and devotion
In the guru and the lord, inseparable.

Receive these offerings
Lord of Pristine Awareness, Wish-granting Gem,
In all the forms you assume,

Along with Lady Glorious Goddess,
Malefactor, Force, Death Lord, and Demon,
And the seventy-five oath-bound and others
Surrounded by all the lordly powers of the three planes
      of existence.

Protect me from threats now, in the future, and in the
      intermediate states.
Build up my stores of food, wealth, and experience.
Make the understanding and practice of the teachings spread.
Set all beings free in full awakening.

MANTRA RECITATION

*om vajra mahakala kching chetra vighana vinayaka hūm hūm pāt
pāt svaha*

TORMA OFFERING

Add *idam balingta kha kha khahi khahi* to the end of Mahakala's mantra and repeat
three times.

Likewise, add *idam balingta kha kha khahi khahi* to each of

bhyo mamo nakmo vitali sindha kulu kulu hūm pāt
om chetra pala vighana hūm pāt
om jina mitra vasham kuru hūm pāt
om traki raja samaya bhyo du dza hūm pāt
om du yog dza mahakala traraksha hūm pāt

repeating each of them three times.

Then repeat

*om shri mahakalaya shasanam upakarinam éshapashima kaloyam idam
ratna trayaya apakarinam yatipratjnya samara satada idam duktram kha
kha khahi khahi mara mara grihana grihana pendha pendha hana hana daha
daha pacha pacha dinamekena maraya hūm pāt*

three times with *idam balingta kha kha khahi khahi* to offer the torma to the host of
oath-bound protectors.

*argham padyam pukpé dhupé aloké gendhé névidya shapda praticha
hūm svaha*

With

om ah hūm

present the inner offering.

PRAISE AND REQUEST

hūm

I bow to fast-acting All Seeing One.
Your feet, graced with anklets, crush Obstacle-Maker.
Great Black One, wearing a tiger-skin skirt,
Your six arms are decorated with snake ornaments.

Your first right holds a chopper, the next a rosary,
And the last violently rattles a hand-drum.
Your left hands hold a skull cup, a trident,
And a noose for catching and binding.

Your face is contorted in wrath, your canines fully bared,
With three fearsome eyes, and hair flaring upwards.
Your forehead is marked with a drop of cinnabar
And Buddha Unshakeable, on your head, is your seal.

You wear a necklace of fifty human heads dripping with blood
And a crown of five skulls inlaid with jewels.
Come from your grove and take these sacrificial offerings.
Please accept this offered sacrifice,

And to my companions and me
Give health, strong lives, and power,
Glory, fame, and good fortune,
And property, wealth, and vast riches.

Give us mastery in pacification,
Enrichment, and other activities.
Keep your commitments and protect us.
Use your abilities and support us.

Eliminate untimely death, illness,
Emotional disturbances, and impediments.
Bad dreams, bad omens,
Bad business, eliminate them all.

Make the world happy, crops grow,
Harvests full, and the Dharma flourish.
Make everything wonderful and joyous;
Bring about all that we wish for.

This is the request for what you want.

Guru and Lord, inseparable,
In you I earnestly take refuge.
May I clear away
Every reaction in every being.

Lord and Guru, inseparable,
In you I earnestly take refuge.
May I clear away
Every impediment for every being.

Repeat three times

Repeat the hundred-syllable mantra three times and the apology prayers.

Whatever mistakes I've made
In mantras, rituals, or activities
Profound and perfect as you are,
I ask you to bear them patiently.

End with aspiration and good fortune prayers.

This simple short sacrificial offering ceremony for The Six-Armed Lord of
Timeless Awareness was composed by Taranatha at Po-trang Gang-Kar at the
request of Nyima Namjé. Translation by Ken McLeod, Los Angeles, California.

Mountain Burnt-Offering

om svasti

This practice of the Mountain Burnt-Offering follows the instructions from Lhatsün Rigdzin's *Life Practices*.

Make a fire full of good fortune, that is, in a clean hearth or container build a fire and burn whatever you have at hand: aromatic woods, resins, medicinal plants, the white and sweet foods, incense, powders, etc. Then sprinkle water on the fire.

om ah hūm

REFUGE

Fierce and potent master of awareness, Pema Tötreng Tsal,
Essence of all sources of refuge in the infinity of existence
        and peace,
In your form, the mandala of buddhas in all experience, potential
        and actual, is complete.
In order to free all beings from existence, I take refuge in you.

Repeat three times.

AWAKENING MIND

I form the intention in order that
In ground presence, the absolute mystery, the sheer clarity of
        timeless awareness,
The distortions of all beings are cleared away.
In awakened body, speech, and mind presence, the four visions
        unfold naturally,
And thus, in the youthful vase body, all beings are free.

Repeat three times.

THE SEVEN-SECTION PRAYER

In being natural awareness, direct and open, I pay homage.
In being sheer clarity, limitless and unfathomable, I present
    offerings.
In being the expanse where all experience, patterned and free, is in
    balance, I confess.
In being the end of experience, beyond mind, I rejoice.
In being the great completion, naturally present, I turn the wheel
    of teaching.
In uprooting patterned existence from its depths, I pray.
In being utterly beyond thinking about the three domains,
    I dedicate.

GENERATION OF SELF

From the unceasing energy that arises from the realm of what is,
    the originally pure,
I take form as Pema Tötreng Tsal, reddish white, in the flower of
    youth.
My form blazes with the splendor of the major and minor marks.
I hold a vajra and skull-cup.
Handsome and majestic in robes and jewelry,
Connection- and awareness-beings combined, in form the union
    of all buddhas,
I am the great and glorious lord of samsara and nirvana.

om ah hūm vajra guru padma siddhi hūm

Repeat a hundred times.

To purify the fire offerings:

ram yam kham

In empty presence, the fire offerings appear — huge clouds rising
      from oceans of pure timeless awareness, wonderfully
      pleasing to every sense, spreading and filling the whole sky.

Charge the fire offerings with the three syllables and three repetitions of the sky-treasure mantra.

om ah hūm

nama sarva tathagatabhyo vishvamukhebhye sarva thakham ungate
      saparana emam gagana kham svaha.

Repeat three times.

Bhrum

In large shining vessels made of precious metals and jewels
The commitment offerings, all that gives pleasure in this world,
Are charged with the energy of the three syllables and become
      liquid timeless awareness,
Exciting the pleasurable sensations of all experience, patterned
      and free.

This offering I present to the gurus, deities, dakinis, and
      protectors,
And all the buddha mandalas in the ten directions,
The local deities of this world, the six kinds of beings, and the
      debt-collecting guests,
Particularly those who would take my life and steal my energy,

The malicious elemental spirits who inflict illness and
      interruptions,
Those who send bad portents and bad omens in dreams and
      symbols,
The eight kinds of unruly demons, the masters of illusions,
Those who have come to collect food, shelter, or wealth,

The forces of darkness and madness, the shades of men and
    women dead and gone,
Ghosts of the murdered, monastery ghosts, house ghosts, ghouls,
    and vampires.
Burnt in these red flames, my debts are paid.
Pleasures rain down, giving everyone exactly what they want.

For as long as the sky is there
I share these infinite sensory pleasures with them.
May the bad and corrupt things I've done and will do,
Appropriating offerings for the Jewels, for the faithful, or for the
    dead,
Be cleared away by this offering fire and burnt offerings.

The tongues of flame touch every particle of what can be or is
    experienced.
May limitless clouds of offerings, as in the aspirations of Ever-
    present Good,
Entirely fill the domains of the awakened.

These tongues of flame blaze with the offering rays of the five
    wisdom lights.
The light fills the six realms down to the depths of the
    deepest hells.
Those who go round and round in the three realms are freed in
    rainbow-light bodies.
May all beings wake up to their awake nature.

om ah hūm

Repeat a hundred or a thousand times or more.

The three dimensions of awakening, pure in their being,
Form the receptacle, an eternal palace of infinite space.

In it, all the matter of the world, potential and actual,
What is true, what is vivid, and what is there,

Melts and becomes liquid awareness,
Its blazing light filling the sky.
The essences of this elixir, drawn from all experience, patterned
        and free,
I share with all who have ever been my guest
From time without beginning until now.

May we acquire the abilities of ground, path, and fruition.
And clear away disruptions in outlook, practice, and behavior.
In the infinite expanse of the wonderful mind of
        Ever-present Good,
May we take hold of eternal being in the youthful vase body.

And when the great sea of samsara is emptied,
May we all become fully awake in the Lotus Web Supreme Realm.

The fire offering of heaps and elements blazes brilliantly with
        radiant health.
The fire offering of white and red awakening mind blazes with
        bliss-emptiness.
The fire offering of emptiness and compassion fills the totality
        of experience.

On the ground of the five vajra lights, all experience, potential or
        actual, patterned or free,
I present the fire offering of naturally present complete awakening.
Old karmic debts — may they be cleared away.
Current breaches — I confess now so that they don't continue.
Future clouding — may I not be caught in that cycle.

I confess all violations, conscious or unconscious,
Of the vows and training
Of individual liberation, awakening being, and awareness holder
And the promises connected with the secret mantra.

May illness, disturbances, distortions, and impurities be
     cleared away.
May the plagues, famines, and wars of this age be eased.

Barbarian attacks on the homeland — stop!
Interruptions to the work of teachers — stop!
Bad portents for the good of the world — stop!
Shortening of life by planets, serpents, or kingly demons — stop!
The eight great threats and sixteen fears — stop!
Bad fortune for me and those around me — stop!
The power and influence of commitment demons and self-interest
     demons — stop!

CONCLUSION

May these offerings please the buddhas.
May they fulfill the desires of the oath-bound.
May they meet the wants of the six kinds of beings.
May they satisfy the owed and the resentful.

May they complete the generation of goodness and awareness.
May they clear away the two distortions and associated
     conditioning.
May we all attain the two pure forms.

Through the power that comes from this bountiful giving
May we awaken naturally in order to help beings.
May all beings who were not freed by earlier buddhas
Be freed by giving.

Any elemental demons who remain here,
Wherever you are, under the ground, on the ground, or in the sky,
Always be loving and kind to all beings
And engage the Dharma day and night.

Through this goodness, may all beings
Complete the generation of goodness and wisdom.
May they attain the two pure forms
That arise from goodness and wisdom.

Like a wish-fulfilling gem or a magic tree,
May I fulfill the hopes of all beings
Without the tensions of effort or strain.
May everyone have the good fortune for their dreams to come true.

Jñana (Dudjom Rinpoche), an old city practitioner worn down by the years, drawing on the practice texts of different lengths that were already available, composed this daily practice liturgy as he was moved to do. Translated by Ken McLeod.

CHAPTER NOTES

INTRODUCTION

pg. 1   *... of ancient India, where it originated, and Tibet ...*

Vajrayana traditions are also found in China, Japan, Korea, Mongolia, and Russia. Traces are found in Indonesia and in Southeast Asia.

pg. 1   *It is complex, multi-faceted, and deeply entwined ...*

Both the complexity and the difficulty are due to these practices having evolved in unbroken lines of transmission over thousands of years, from their probable inception in shamanic practices to the formal religions they became, and from there to their appropriation and integration into paths of mystical practice. Even at this distant remove, when you practice Vajrayana, you are, in effect, following the way a shaman may have taken — connecting with a deity as a source of power and abilities, making that deity come alive and active in your life, discovering through that deity levels of attention and awareness that seem beyond human experience, and from there, finding a relationship with life, a way to live in mystery, that is free of struggle.

Practice traditions emerged based on the principal deities in Indian religious culture at that time — Avalokiteshvara, Tara, Shiva, Kali and many others. Each of these deities was the central figure of what today we would regard as a religion in its own right. These ancient deities were the source of the major tantras, where the word tantra refers to the collected teachings and practices associated with a particular deity. To take up deity practice was to take one of these deities as one's personal god.

Exactly how these tantras fused with Buddhist principles, we don't know. One possibility is that mystical aspirants who left the monasteries to search for more vibrant methods of practice took their Buddhist training with them. They learned contemplative, magical, and energy transformation methods from sorcerers and magicians. Then they adapted and applied these methods to their own questions and interests, particularly the aim of awakening based in the Mahayana principles of buddha nature, bodhicitta or awakening mind, and the union of compassion and emptiness.

Nor do we know exactly how these religious and sorcery cults evolved into the body of practices we now know as Vajrayana, but we do know that practices from one tantra were often combined with practices from other tantras. As far as we can tell, there was no system as such, just a plethora of different methods and approaches that had evolved in the rich religious culture of ancient

India. Individual practitioners often studied with a number of teachers and then passed on the combination of practices they deemed most helpful to each of their students.

pg. 2   *... from India to Tibet in two waves...*

Buddhism came to Tibet in two waves. The first wave, the Old School or Nyingma, is based on practices from northwest India in the 8th century. The second wave, the New School (Sakya, Kadam, Kagyu, and others), is based on practices largely from central and eastern India in the 11th and 12th centuries. Tibet provided an environment in which the teachings that were brought from India could be studied and practiced without dilution. Over the centuries, lines of transmission crisscrossed as practitioners sought out methods and teachings that led them to the understanding they sought. Teachings and practices were constantly refined, and the methods that proved most effective in one generation were transmitted to the next.

Repeatedly over the course of the last thousand years, the greatest minds of the Tibetan tradition (Longchenpa, Butön, Taranatha, and Jamgön Kongtrül to name just four) sought to bring order to the mass of practices and teachings that Tibet had inherited. But Vajrayana, being a product of evolution and cross-fertilization, defies any attempt to impose a rigorous taxonomy. As in biology, whatever the classification system, there is always a duck-billed platypus.

pg. 3   *The Meaning of Vajrayana*

The correct spelling with diacritical marks in English is Vajrayāna. For ease of reading, however, I omit diacritical marks except where they are an aid to pronunciation.

pg. 6   *...a mediated completion phase...*

There are two approaches to completion phase practice. The first is unmediated completion phase, the direct entry into empty clear knowing through the intentional dissolution of the experience of being the deity. The second is mediated completion phase, an entry into empty clear knowing mediated by energy transformation practices such as inner heat (tumo), magical apparition, sheer clarity, or dream.

pg. 8   *...Shangpa and Karma Kagyu...*

Tibetan Buddhism evolved into four principal lineages, the Nyingma from the first wave of translation, and the Sakya, Kadam, and Kagyu from the second wave. The Kadam was gradually absorbed by the other traditions, but was then revised and reformulated as the Gelug tradition in the 14th century. The many Kagyupa lineages have a common source in the 11th century translator Marpa. One of these, the Karma Kagyu, traces its beginning back to the 12th century in the person of Karmapa Düsum Khyenpa. Although nominally a Kagyupa tradition, the Shangpa Kagyupa is a completely separate lineage established by Khyungpo Naljor in the 11th century.

pg. 8   … *after I left the three-year retreat …*

The three-year retreat program taught by Kalu Rinpoche was established by Jamgön Kongtrul in the 19th century in Eastern Tibet. The curriculum included the common and special groundwork practices (ngöndro), mahamudra, Mahayana Mind Training and taking and sending (tonglen), about one year of deity practice, about one year on the Six Practices of each of Niguma, Naropa, and Sukhasiddhi, protector practice, the practice of Cutting (Chö), and the practices of Hayagriva and White Tara.

pg. 9   *…following exactly in their footsteps.*

Do not seek to follow in the footsteps of the wise. Seek what they sought.
— Kūkai (Kōbō-Daishi) (774–835)

This quotation is often incorrectly attributed to the Japanese poet Basho. Basho himself attributes it to Kūkai, the founder of the Japanese Vajrayana tradition of Shingon.

See https://internalgongfu.blogspot.com/2018/11/seek-what-masters -sought-kukai-kobo.html?m=1

CHAPTER I

pg. 11   *"Empty experience," I thought to myself …*

See glossary entry for *empty experience*.

pg. 11   *… energy transformation …*

Transformation is a process that takes place spontaneously when attention at a higher level of energy is brought to bear on experience at a lower level of energy. Energy transformation can take place with sensory experience, emotional reactions, levels of attention, the four immeasurables, conceptual knowing, and so on. In the presence of the higher level of energy, the reactive processes associated with the experience cannot play out as usual. They disintegrate and their energy is transformed to a higher level. See Ken McLeod, *Wake Up to Your Life*, pg. 308ff.

pg 12   *… direct knowing …*

Direct knowing is the third of four levels of understanding in the Tibetan traditions of Buddhist practice. The first is intellectual or conceptual understanding (Tib. *go ba*). The second is experiential understanding (Tib. *nyams*), usually precipitated by surges of energy as reactive patterns disintegrate. This level of understanding is unstable as it depends on fluxes of energy. However, it can give the practitioner a taste of real understanding. The third level is direct knowing

(Tib. *rtogs pa*), a shift in the practitioner's system into a direct, non-conceptual knowing. According to traditional teaching it is stable and irreversible. However, if it is not practiced and cultivated, both its presence and influence can and does wane. The fourth level is release (Tib. *grol ba*), in which the salient reactive patterns have lost their power to condition experience and direct knowing comes into operation whenever circumstances call for it.

pg. 12   *Aspirations for Mahamudra*

For an English translation of this prayer, see https://unfetteredmind.org/aspirations-for-mahamudra/

The Great Seal is an English translation of the Sanskrit Mahamudra, The Great Middle Way is Mahāmadhyamaka, and The Great Completion is Mahāsaṅdhi or Dzogchen.

pg. 12   *...each of these names was a kind of pointing-out instruction...*

For instance, in this prayer from Karma Chakmé's *Mountain Dharma*, he gives pointing-out instructions for direct knowing in each of the principal Mahamudra traditions:

When you look inwards, there is nothing to be seen.
Experience drops into naked ordinary knowing.
Looking outwards, everything is like a rainbow:
While what appears is clear, it is in essence empty.
Appearance and existence arise like magic.

Whatever thoughts of the five poisons arise,
Look at their essence and they release on their own.
This is the instruction for the natural release of the five poisons.
Whatever kinds of happiness and suffering arise,
Look at their essence and they release on their own.
This is the mahamudra of making all tastes equal.

Whatever disturbing and frightening experiences arise,
Look at their essence and they release on their own.
This is the mahamudra of the cutting ground (Chö).
Whatever forms of struggle arise,
Look at their essence and they release on their own.
This is the holy instruction of calming suffering.

Mind is free from existence or non-existence, order or chaos.
This is the holy instruction of the great middle way.

There is no experience that is not complete in the mind.
This is the holy instruction of the great completion.

The mind of the Victorious One, your own mind,
And the mind of every being are in essence one.
This is the view that samsara and nirvana are inseparable.

Place your mind without trying to cultivate something:
This is the instruction of naked ordinary knowing.

Place your mind without looking or something looked for:
This is the practice of mahamudra.

pg. 13   *... in a field of energy.*

When you are in the presence of your teacher, you may experience the transmission of energy, clarity, or emptiness in different ways—as a heightened clarity or awareness, as a deep peace, as a freedom from emotional reactivity, as a feeling of intense love or devotion, as a shift in sensory perception, as a charge that makes the hair on the back of your neck stand up, or as nothing special at all.

pg. 13   *This is transmission.*

Transmission can take place so quietly and simply that it is almost as if nothing has happened. The next day, or the next week, you realize that you are clearer and less reactive or that your meditation has changed in a way you cannot explain. It can also be such a radical shift that your life is never the same. Whatever your experience, a seed is planted, a seed that grows and matures through practice.

pg. 13   *A meditation deity* (yidam *in Tibetan)...*

The closest analogy in Western spirituality is probably a patron saint in Catholicism. Your deity embodies the spiritual qualities and understanding to which you aspire. Through prayer and ritual you build a relationship with your deity. Through this relationship you discover the potential for those qualities in you. As the relationship deepens, your deity purifies you and your life. Your life is progressively emptied of any investment of self and you gradually become the deity. When you are able to experience birth and death as the deity, the distortions of reactivity and confusion dissolve, your ordinary sense of self drops away, and you really are the deity, with all its abilities, powers, and qualities. This transformation of experience changes your understanding of what life is, of what you are, and of how to live.

pg. 13   *Vajrayana is described as the path of result.*

In Vajrayana, methods and results are often reversed when compared with other approaches to spiritual practice. For instance, in deity practice, the non-conceptual knowing that is the result of stability and insight in other paths becomes the path: the deity is non-conceptual knowing and you are the deity. Conversely, through deity practice, you develop the stability and power of attention and insight into the nature of experience that are understood as methods in other approaches. In the same way, the end result of life is death. In deity practice, that result becomes your method of practice: you die to your ordinary life in order to live as the deity.

pg. 14   *... you are introduced to your deity through four empowerments ...*

The four empowerments are present implicitly or explicitly in virtually every deity empowerment ritual.

In the vase empowerment, your teacher and the empowerment deities pour the elixir of awareness over you and into you, anointing and confirming you as the deity. The vase empowerment is simultaneously a purification, a consecration, and a transmission of power. It plants a seed of experience in you. You are able to be the deity in the deity's world and you practice being the deity, saying the deity's mantra, and resting in the deity's mind. Then one day, during meditation or when you are going about your day, the world arises like a dream, like an illusion, like an enchantment. You are perfectly functional, but the world and you are never the same. The spell of the seeming solidity of sensory experience has been broken. That is the actual vase empowerment.

For the secret empowerment, in some rituals you are shown a picture of feces and urine — coded or secret language for emotional reactivity — and you are told to enjoy them. Enjoy them? Your mind balks at the thought, and in that momentary opening a second seed is planted, a seed that points to the emptiness in emotional reactions. This seed is the possibility of seeing the emptiness in anger, desire, pride, or other reactive emotions. When you are the deity, these reactive emotions have less to hook onto. At some point, you experience these reactions as having no ground. Through this experience, you come to know the mystical potential, the freedom, hidden in reactive emotions. The spell of their seeming solidity has been broken and you have received (or attained) the secret empowerment.

For the wisdom-awareness empowerment, in some traditions you are given a cut diamond. The way it reflects, refracts, and diffracts light plants a third seed, a seed that grows into knowing the radiance, dynamism, and play of direct awareness. In other traditions, you are given a circle that is half black and half white, planting a seed that points you to an awareness that is beyond polarities, and with it the possibility of knowing all experience, pleasant or unpleasant, patterned or free, transcendent or mundane, to be movement in mind. These understandings break the spell of any idea of transcendence, and with that shift you have attained the wisdom-awareness empowerment.

The full name of this empowerment is the empowerment of timeless awareness that arises through connection with a wisdom partner. Through mastery of the channels, winds, and vital essences, you are able to generate similitudes of timeless awareness by transforming sexual energy with an imagined or actual partner. Through these experiences, you come to know that all generated experiences are movements in mind. With this understanding you are able to let go of the four spiritual ideals—everlasting life, eternal bliss, transcendent purity, and universal selfhood.

The fourth empowerment, the word empowerment, plants a seed of direct awareness. There is little ceremony. Your teacher elicits a shift into direct awareness in you—by joining with your mind, making a symbolic gesture, or giving you verbal instruction. Whether you experience anything explicitly depends on many factors—your natural ability, your relationship with your teacher, your practice and training, and chance, to name a few. As your practice matures, however, a day may come when something shifts and you know, to the very core of your being, the timeless awareness that has always been there. With this understanding, the spell of the solidity of practice is broken. You know there is no doer and there is nothing to be done, you have attained the fourth empowerment, and you are able to practice mahamudra and dzogchen.

pg. 15   *The Teacher's Touch*

This scenario is about teacher-union practice, or guru yoga, a practice in which your mind joins with your teacher's mind, your heart with your teacher's heart. Many different kinds of experience may arise. The one described here is a way in which the power and energy of devotion moves you beyond the conceptual mind and into a different way of experiencing.

pg. 17   *Deity Dreams*

The first scenario is based on the Mati tradition of White Manjushri, the second on Green Tara, and the third on Chakrasamvara. Each dream starts with an idealized description of deity meditation. The second part of each dream describes the shifts that the practice may induce in life.

pg. 17   *... eight white elephants ...*

The eight elephants represent the eight consciousnesses (the six consciousnesses associated with each of the six senses including thinking, the emotional mind, and the basis-of-everything consciousness). Manjushri, the bodhisattva of awakened intelligence, represents mind nature, a non-conceptual knowing that differs from the knowing in which subject and object are separate.

pg. 18   *It is green...*

Green Tara, the embodiment of how awakened compassion acts in the world. In this capacity, she operates both as a protector and as a personal deity.

pg. 19   ... *simultaneously male and female* ...

Chakrasamvara in union with Vajrayogini. This pair is a central deity or yidam in several traditions of Tibetan Buddhism and is closely associated with the transformation of sexual energy into an intense bliss. That bliss, in turn, is the basis for a high level of attention that penetrates and opens to the emptiness of all experience.

pg. 20   ... *charming, firm and direct; unpredictable, tough, and intimidating; and calm, understanding, and persuasive.*

The nine expressions of semi-wrathful deities, expressed in three groups of three that correspond to body, speech, and mind.

pg. 20   *Protector power*

This scenario is loosely based on the practice of the Six-Armed Mahakala or Lord of Timeless Awareness, the principal protector of the Shangpa tradition.

pg. 20   *Difficult situations are no longer as difficult.*

What follows is an informal description of how the four awakening actions might manifest in actual life. The four awakening actions can be regarded as four stages of conflict, beginning with approaching the conflict calmly, then expansively, then forcefully, then, if necessary, terminating the situation in which the conflict arises.

pg. 24   *Groundwork*

The literal meaning of the Tibetan term *sngon 'gro* (pron. ngöndro) is *what goes before*, i.e., preparation. However, it is often translated as preliminary. A set of groundwork practices is intended to prepare the practitioner for higher level spiritual practice, and there are several kinds of groundwork.

The general groundwork is a set of four meditations from Mahayana Mind Training—the precious human birth, death and impermanence, karma as genesis and result, and the shortcomings of samsara. These meditations are intended to shift the student's attention from the conventional to the spiritual. They are common to all traditions of Tibetan Buddhism.

In addition, each tradition has one or more special groundwork practices for advanced energy transformation practice and for direct awareness practice. While there are differences from tradition to tradition, the set usually consists of five practices: prostrations while taking refuge, generating awakening mind (bodhicitta), Vajrasattva purification practice, a symbolic offering of the universe according to Indian and Tibetan cosmology, and teacher-union practice.

CHAPTER 2

pg. 29 *Niguma, an 11th century Indian mystic ...*

For more on Niguma, see *Niguma, Lady of Illusion.* In this book Sarah Harding has brought together everything in the historical record about Niguma.

pg. 32 *Like many practices in the Tibetan tradition ...*

Practices are often based on a teacher's vision, a dream, an encounter with a historic figure or a deity, or an experience of awakening.

pg. 33 *What is the basis for your faith?*

The first verse in this practice is about faith based in reason, the second about faith based in yearning, and the third about faith based in clarity.

pg. 33 *... the abbot of Bodhgaya ...*

Bodhgaya is where Buddha Shakyamuni experienced his awakening. It became the center of the Buddhist world in India. As such, the position of Abbot of Bodhgaya was a very high-ranking position. After Buddhism faded away in India, the temple at Bodhgaya was lost in jungle and was only rediscovered by British archeologists in the 19th century. Today, virtually all major Buddhist traditions have temples and monasteries there.

pg. 36 *You are in a charnel ground, in Sosa Grove.*

The charnel ground where Khyungpo Naljor was told he might find Niguma.

pg. 38 *The flesh-eating dakinis are licking their chops.*

In Indian mythology, a dakini (she who flies in the sky) are female spirits that can possess, i.e., devour, a practitioner. If the practitioner recognizes that these spirits are his or her own mind, the activity of the dakinis becomes the play of timeless awareness. See *Wake Up to Your Life,* pg. 213ff.

pg. 42 *In 1971 I met the Sixteenth Karmapa ...*

The Karmapa line of incarnate teachers goes back to the 12th century. It was the first to be recognized in Tibet. Since then, the Karmapas have been the spiritual heads of the Karma Kagyu lineage in every generation.

pg. 42 *Was he talking about blind faith ...*

Blind faith is not faith at all. It is belief, an emotional stance based in a set view. Everything that happens, good or bad, even evidence to the contrary, is interpreted to conform to the belief.

pg. 42   ... *faith has to be unchanging* ...

Faith is a kind of knowing. Faith means that whatever you encounter, you meet it, open to it, see into it, and accept what you see or understand, even if it upsets or negates prior assumptions, understandings, or deeply held views. Faith suggests, if not reveals, that the reasoning mind is not the only way to know. It is not rational, but neither is it irrational. Because it comes from a place that does not use or need to use reason, rational and irrational do not apply.

pg. 45   *Doing nothing in mind is the essence of mahamudra.*

The similarities between the knowing implicit in faith and the knowing uncovered in mahamudra are too compelling to ignore. In the Shangpa tradition the knowing in mahamudra is described as:

Too close—you don't see it.
Too deep—you don't recognize it.
Too easy—you don't trust it.
Too noble—you don't accept it.

Exactly the same might be said of faith. It is closer than your own shadow. It goes deeper than you can possibly plumb. It is so clear and simple that you have no idea of its provenance. And there is a nobility in it that leaves you silent.

pg. 45   *Chenrezi*

Chenrezi (Tib. *spyan ras gzigs*, Skt. Avalokiteshvara) is the embodiment of awakened compassion. His original name meant *he who hears the suffering of the world*, but this gradually changed to *he who looks over the world*. His mantra *om mani padme hūm* is probably the most recited mantra in the Tibetan tradition. Chenrezi became the androgynous deity Kuan Yin in China and the female deity Kannon in Japan.

pg. 46   ... *is more than a person* ...

That what you are praying to is more than a person is made explicit in the practice of teacher-union. In the Kagyu tradition, you see your teacher as the primordial buddha Vajradhara, in the Nyingma tradition as the founding teacher Guru Padmasambhava, in the Gelug tradition as the founding teacher Tsongkhapa, and so on. In teacher-union practice, your teacher stands for all your teachers and all the teachers of all the lineages through which you have received instruction or guidance.

pg. 46   ... *what is exemplified in my teacher—mind nature, direct awareness* ...

See https://unfetteredmind.org/recognizing-mind-as-the-guru/

pg. 52   *... he said it was* zhi mé tsa tral *...*

Tib. gzhi med rtsa bral

pg. 54   *Nor is there any absolute or ultimate truth, state of perfection, ideal, or final*
             achievement.

Teachings in different spiritual traditions on the creation and end of the world,
God, karma, rebirth, emptiness, buddha nature, Brahma, Atman, heaven, hell,
and so on are frameworks that provide individuals and societies with ways to
understand, explain, and give direction to their lives. The same holds for sci-
entific views, astronomy, biology, quantum mechanics, or neurology, different
schools of philosophy, and any number of disciplines, whether an art, an ath-
letic endeavor, or a profession.

CHAPTER 3

pg. 56   *... you develop certain powers ...*

In Vajrayana there are two kinds of powers: ordinary powers and spiritual powers. Ordinary powers are such magical powers as clairvoyance, telekinesis, the
ability to become invisible, or the ability to move instantly from one place to
another. Spiritual powers are qualities such as determination, compassion, or
faith — powers that are important in spiritual practice. The special or highest
power is mahamudra or dzogchen, that is, the power or ability to rest awareness in what arises without being pulled into interaction with it.

pg. 56   *Of the thousands of empowerments ...*

According to Tsele Natsok Rangdrol, there are 2440 different kinds of empowerments in the Nyingma tradition alone. See *Empowerment and the Path of Liberation,* trans. Erik Schmidt.

pg. 56   *... through the empowerment ritual.*

The empowerment ritual presented here is more accurately called a permission ritual.

In the Tibetan tradition, there are five transmission rituals. Beginning with the
simplest, they are entrustment, authorization, permission, energy transmission, and mystical initiation.

In the entrustment ritual (*bka' btad,* pron. ka té)), the teacher directs a deity to
watch over and take care of the student.

The authorization ritual (*rlung,* pron. lūng) is a formal reading of a practice text
related to the deity of the student. Authorization rituals are not limited to practice texts. They are given for almost every kind of text in the Tibetan tradition.

Permission rituals (*rjes gnang*, pron. jé nang) comprise the largest category of transmission ceremonies. In this kind of ritual, the student is formally introduced to the deity and invested with the energy of the primordial deity. With this formal introduction, the student has permission to become the deity, repeat the deity's mantra, cultivate the qualities of the deity, and become familiar with the essence of the deity, namely, timeless awareness.

In the energy transmission ritual (*byin brlabs*, pron. jin lab) and the mystical initiation ritual (*dbang chen*, pron. wang chen), the student receives the four empowerments explicitly—the vase empowerment, the secret empowerment, the wisdom-awareness empowerment, and the fourth or word empowerment. The principal difference between the energy transmission ritual and the mystical empowerment ritual is that the latter includes an additional empowerment, the vajra-master empowerment, which plants the seed for the student to become a teacher in his or her own right.

pg. 57   *... the long Vajrasattva mantra ...*

A primordial buddha associated with purification, he may also be taken as a yidam or personal deity. The hundred-syllable mantra of Vajrasattva is the purification mantra used in many traditions of groundwork.

pg. 57   *... a baton decorated with peacock feathers ...*

Peacocks are able to ingest and digest foods that would kill other animals, making them a suitable symbol for the transformative powers of Vajrayana practice.

pg. 57   *Great Compassion*

One of many epithets for Avalokiteshvara. The adjective great often endows the person or quality with mystical significance. Thus, Great Compassion means that the compassion of Avalokiteshvara is not a conceptual, ordinary, or conventional compassion, but a non-referential compassion, a mystical compassion.

pg. 58   *Vajrayana, like all Mahayana practice, ...*

In the Tibetan tradition, the Mahayana, the great or universal way, is divided into Sutra Mahayana and Tantra Mahayana. In the path of sutras, you nurture the qualities that mature into awakened knowing. In the path of tantras, you give direct expression to the awakened knowing that has been present in you from time without beginning.

pg. 58   *All experience is naturally pure...*

In the Tibetan tradition, in deference to India from where Buddhism came to Tibet, all mantras are said in Sanskrit. In more than a few instances, it is helpful to know what they mean.

pg. 61   *... the channels, energy, and vital essences ...*

In mediated completion phase practice, the practitioner uses meditations, breathing exercises, and physical movements to straighten out the knots and blockages in the channels (Tib. *rtsa*), restore the free flow of energy (Tib. *rlung*), and activate vital essences (Tib. *thig le*) in the key centers of the body. These practices generate similitudes of awakening, notably experiences of bliss, clarity, and non-thought. Such practices belong to the path of method. See Chapter 6 for guidelines for working with energy.

pg. 64   *Another is energy.*

The way a flame is transmitted from one candle to another is one analogy for how energy is transmitted. Energy from the lit candle creates a field of heat which melts the wax in the wick of the unlit candle until it vaporizes, reaches its ignition point, and spontaneously bursts into flame. Ideally, the teacher creates an energy field in which some understanding, energy, and experience of the deity comes across to the student. In practice, when you receive an initiation, you may not be aware that something has changed inside. Just because you do not feel anything or think that anything has happened does not mean that something has not changed. On the other hand, there are factors that do prevent transmission. The student may not respond to the energy field. The energy field triggers something in the student and he or she shuts down. The teacher may not have enough power or ability to create an energy field. The teacher and student may not resonate with each other, or resonate in a way that is problematic, and so forth.

pg. 66   *An empowerment ritual is theatre, a play in which every aspect ...*

The play can be seen as an allegory of your own mind. The mythic world of the empowerment with White Tara, your teacher, you, and everyone else is your mind. Your teacher as White Tara is the awakened aspect of your mind. The shrine deity, the primordial White Tara, is the form that timeless awareness— your own mind in the deepest sense—takes to help you awaken. Together, the awakened aspect of your mind and your mind in the deepest sense, timeless awareness, reveal what is possible, and the seeds of those possibilities are planted in you.

pg. 67   *... samaya, the ethics of Vajrayana ...*

Samaya is the Sanskrit word for commitment. It carries the sense of both loyalty and connection. It is the basis of the ethics of Vajrayana. Its Tibetan equivalent is *dam tshig* (pron. dam tsik). In the Vajrayana context, samaya is the commitment to go empty in everything you experience, to recognize and touch the mystical dimension in every aspect of life.

The three principal areas where samaya applies are the teacher-student relationship, your relationship with your personal deity, and your relationship with the protectors and dakinis.

As a teacher, samaya means that you see the student as embodying the potential to be awake—a potential buddha. Your commitment or samaya is to nurture that potential. Your primary gesture is compassion, not the compassion that seeks to alleviate suffering, but the compassion that seeks an end to suffering. You seek to bring the student to the point that he or she no longer struggles with the exigencies of life, internally or externally. As a teacher, you realize that aim by helping the student become free from the tyranny of reactivity and confusion through knowing and experiencing the utter groundlessness of experience. As a teacher, your connection with being awake is to guide the student in that direction. If you wittingly or unwittingly seek to satisfy your own wants or needs through a student, be they financial, social, romantic, political, or sexual, you are indulging your own reactivity and confusion and have fallen out of your connection with being awake. If you do not recognize or acknowledge that you have fallen out of that connection and return to it, you have stepped out of both the teacher-student relationship and your own commitment or samaya.

As a student, samaya means that you see the teacher as exemplifying what it is to be present and awake. Your primary gesture is devotion and respectful appreciation for your teacher and his or her understanding and ability. Your commitment is to make use of your teacher's instructions. If you use your teacher to feel special, to have a special relationship, or to escape the mundane dissatisfactions in life, you have also stepped out of the teacher-student relationship. If, for whatever reason, you are clear that you can no longer study with or learn from a teacher, you thank him or her for what you have received and take your leave.

In deity practice, samaya means to experience life as the deity. If you are practicing being the embodiment of awakened compassion (Avalokiteshvara or Kuan Yin), you feel infinite compassion for all beings, and you are willing to plunge into the depths of your own reactive patterns (the hell realms of anger and hate, for instance) if by doing so, you can help even one person or one part of you wake up. Your commitment is to touch non-referential compassion in your heart until it permeates everything you experience.

The female deities known as dakinis are how mind moves in empty experience. The essence of the commitment here is to trust the non-conceptual knowing of empty experience—knowing what to do in a given situation without relying on the conceptual mind. Where that knowing comes from is a mystery, but it is clear, precise, balanced, effective, and complete—the five aspects of timeless awareness.

The nightmarish forms of most protectors reflect the forces stirred up in difficult situations — the dark primitive forces that go into operation when we feel threatened. The commitment here is to experience those difficult situations in empty experience. There is a wakefulness even in these dark forces. You meet whatever life throws at you in empty experience as the four awakening activities — pacification, enrichment, magnetization, and destruction — arise naturally.

CHAPTER 4

pg. 70   *... the illusory reality of sensory experience, of emotions, of transcendent experiences, and of control.*

We live under the sway of four enchantments that keep us from acknowledging that everything — sensory experience, emotions, thoughts, or beliefs — comes and goes. The first enchantment is the enchantment of form, that the world we experience with our senses is solid and real. Second is the enchantment of emotions and feelings, believing and trusting them even though they are only waves in mind. The third is the enchantment of transcendence, that it is somehow possible to transcend the human condition and enjoy everlasting life, transcendent purity, eternal bliss, or universal selfhood. The last is the enchantment of control, that we are in some way masters of our destiny. Through Vajrayana practice you come to see how these enchantments arise and how to dispel them.

pg. 70   *... oral authorization for the practice text ...*

Oral authorization is one of three elements in the transmission of deity practice from teacher to student. The three are: empowerment, oral authorization, and instruction. Empowerment ripens or plants a seed of experience in the student. Oral authorization supports the student. Instruction in the practice provides the student with the means to find freedom from reactivity and confusion.

In the oral authorization, the teacher reads the text aloud to the student, transmitting both the content and energy of the practice. Before the invention of paper and printing, texts were very rare, especially in India where dried palm leaves were used for books. Oral authorization was important because it was often the only time that the student could learn the full scope of practices associated with his or her deity.

pg. 71   *Mastery of the Deathless*

This practice text was composed by the 19th century master Jamgön Kongtrul. In it he brings together five different lineages of White Tara transmissions. He named it *Mastery of the Deathless: A simple daily practice for Lady Wishing Wheel.* Lady is a female honorific, just as Lord is a male honorific. Wishing Wheel is one of the many names for White Tara, the wheel being a symbol of power in Indian mythology, the wishing signifying that the wheel has the power to fulfill your wishes. The title Mastery of the Deathless is a double-entendre—White Tara herself is associated with long life, and through White Tara, you come to know that which is beyond death. This White Tara text is the text for the final month of practice in the three-year retreat. It includes most of the major elements you find in a more elaborate practice text, albeit in abbreviated form. A translation of the complete text is included in the appendices.

pg. 71 … *Jamgön Kongtrul* …

Jamgön Kongtrul the Great was a 19th century teacher in Eastern Tibet. Though recognized at an early age for both for his intellect and his spiritual talent, he was designated an incarnate lama (tulku) largely for political reasons. He, along with two other teachers, Khyentse Wangpo and Chokgyur Lingpa, worked hard to preserve the often fragile lines of transmission of thousands of teachings. Kongtrul's contribution to this effort was five massive collections of teachings, known today as *The Five Treasuries* (Tib. *rdzod.lnga*).

pg. 72 … *her and her heirs* …

The bodhisattvas who have come to awakening through White Tara.

pg. 72 *vajra samaja*

This spell means "Come here, Vajra!"

pg. 74 *om shunyata jñana vajra svabhava atma koñ ham*

I am empty timeless awareness

The main part of deity practice begins with this spell. There are many kinds of spells in Vajrayana: protection spells, transformation spells, healing spells, rain spells, wealth spells, and spells for good or bad luck. This spell, however, is an enchantment-breaking spell. It breaks the enchantment that binds you to samsara, the cycle of confusion and emotional reaction.

Most deity practices open with one of two spells. One means "I am empty timeless awareness." A few extra syllables are included, i.e., the customary opening *om* and *vajra* for emphasis. (It is Vajrayana after all.) The other spell is "All experience is naturally pure, I am naturally pure." It refers to a purity that embraces both the pure and the impure, that is, a purity beyond the conceptual mind—essentially a synonym for emptiness.

Both spells stop the mind, the first by pointing to a knowing that cannot be put into words, the second to an emptiness that is beyond the conceptual mind.

pg. 74 *That way of experiencing, that way of knowing, is everything.*

In technical parlance, the first moment of knowing is called the attention of suchness. It refers to the indescribable groundlessness you experience when mind stops.

In this context, attention is used to translate the Sanskrit word *samadhi*.

The second moment, when you experience the clarity of emptiness, is called the attention of radiance. Radiance in this context refers to the clarity aspect of mind nature. If emptiness is analogous to space, clarity is analogous to light.

The third moment, when you experience a knowing that cannot be put into words, is the genesis of the deity. Again in technical parlance, this is called the attention of genesis. This is what becomes the deity, analogous to the way an acorn becomes an oak tree.

pg. 76 *The sound takes form as a huge dome.*

As in almost all magic rituals, the first step is to generate a protection circle to shield you and the magic you do from distractions and disruptive forces—the workings of the conceptual mind with its limitations, conditioned propensities, and emotional reactions. The protection circle is made of vajras, the vajras representing how non-conceptual knowing is beyond change and corruption.

pg. 77 *... the thirty-seven factors of awakening ...*

The thirty-seven factors are common to virtually all traditions of Buddhism. They comprise a description of the qualities that culminate in buddhahood or full awakening. The Tibetan presentation can be found in numerous texts now in English. See Sarah Harding's *Niguma, Lady of Illusion*, page 53, Gampopa's *The Jewel Ornament of Liberation*, or https://www.lotsawahouse.org/tibetan-masters/patrul-rinpoche/stages-and-path

pg. 77 *... Tara's seed syllable ...*

In the parlance of Western traditions of magic, the seed syllable is a sigil, a symbol of the magician's intended outcome.

pg. 77 *Now you take birth as White Tara, your body vivid, clear, and empty ...*

There are many variations in this birth process, from instantaneously becoming the deity to the five-fold purification. They generally fall into four categories that correspond to the different ways beings are born according to the medieval Indian understanding: instantaneously as in the god and hell realms, from heat and moisture as in the insect realm, from an egg as in birds and reptiles, or from a womb as in human beings.

Similarly, there are variations in how the deity's world comes into being. The most elaborate go through the emergence of the whole cosmos, from the five elements of space, wind, fire, water, and earth, the formation of the cosmos according to Indian cosmology, and the formation of the palace. The least elaborate is that the deity and the deity's world all arise instantaneously.

The form of the deity's palace also varies. In the White Manjushri, it is an island in the middle of a lake. In White Tara and many other deities, it is a palace made of crystal and rainbows. In the shorter versions of Chakrasamvara, there is no palace as such, just an eight-petalled lotus with the attendant dakinis and four vases with skull cups sitting on top of each. In the more elaborate versions, the lotus sits in the central hall of an ornate palace in which each architectural feature represents one of the thirty-seven factors of awakening.

pg. 83   *… though it is also translated as pure experience, pure appearance, or pure vision …*

The word pure can be understood in two different ways. The more common usage is a state free from contaminants—pure gold, for instance. The word purify in this context means to remove impurities. In Buddhist mystical practice, however, the word pure refers to something that goes beyond pure and impure, or, to put it another way, that includes both the pure and the impure. As such, it is a synonym for emptiness. In mystical practice, we are not seeking a state of purity in which no impurity is present. Nor are we seeking a state of emptiness in which nothing arises. The word purify in this context does not mean to remove impurities, but to empty experience of the investment of self. It would probably be more accurate to call it emptification, but no such word exists in English.

CHAPTER 5

pg. 89   *There are layers of deeper magic at work here …*

The origins of both Buddhist and Hindu tantra are a bit obscure, but they seem to have developed at approximately the same time from formalized systems of magic practiced by sorcerers and magicians. Their deities were originally the central figures of distinct religions, some of which, such as Shaivism or the cult of Kali, are practiced to this day.

pg. 90   *… buddhas of the five families …*

The five buddha families are the five aspects of timeless awareness: mirror-like, balancing, distinguishing, effective, and all-encompassing.

pg. 94   *Radiation-absorption is a method of energy transformation …*

Every deity practice includes at least one form of this sending out–drawing in or radiation–absorption. As Avalokiteshvara, for instance, you radiate energy to the six kinds of beings, transform their anger and jealousy, their pride and stupidity, and their greed and desire into the corresponding aspects of timeless awareness, and then draw that in. As Hayagriva, you radiate millions of miniature Hayagrivas, like sparks flying off a grindstone. They instantly annihilate every emotional reaction, leaving a field of transformed energy that you then absorb. Sometimes the light you send to the buddhas carries offerings and offering goddesses, and you draw in their energy as forms of the deity, syllables of the mantra, and the implements they hold—body, speech, and mind. Sometimes the light to sentient beings takes the form of particular buddhas, or forms of the deity of different colors, and you draw in the energy of the corresponding transformation.

pg. 95   *It is as if another being has come into you ...*

The attention-being is the third of the three facets of a deity: the connection-being, the awareness-being, and the attention-being.

pg. 98   *Taking and sending (tonglen) from Mahayana Mind-Training ...*

In taking and sending, you take in the struggles of others and send out your own peace and joy, letting the taking in and sending out ride on the inhalation and exhalation of the breath. See *The Great Path of Awakening,* Jamgön Kongtrul's meditation manual for this practice.

CHAPTER 6

pg. 109   *... maybe just a glimmer at first, as if you are in a dream ...*

This is a subtle shift from awareness and experience as being separate to awareness and experience not being separate. In the former, you experience a world out there and awareness is in you. In the latter, you know that what you experience is your mind, as you do when you are aware that you are dreaming.

pg. 111   *... deity with which you have the strongest connection.*

Each of the Six Practices was originally associated with a particular deity. Over time, instead of practicing six different deities for the Six Practices, students did all Six Practices with one deity, the deity with which they had the strongest connection.

While the four levels of tantra—ritual tantra, behavior tantra, union tantra, and supreme union tantra—are often used to classify deities, practices, and texts, my teacher regarded the four levels as degrees of connection with your deity. In ritual tantra you regard the deity as an ideal, as an embodiment of the qualities to which you aspire. In behavior tantra, you regard the deity as a peer, in whose company those qualities grow in you. In union tantra, you regard the deity as your own mind and you connect to those qualities through symbols. In supreme union tantra, you are the deity, the deity is you, and those qualities are present and active in you.

Ideally, when you engage mediated completion phase practices such as inner heat, magical apparition, dream, or sheer clarity, you have had some experience of being the deity at the level of supreme union tantra. One important reason is that when you are the deity, patterns of emotional reaction and conceptual knowing are not able to function as they do ordinarily and they are less likely to generate problems in the energy transformation practices of mediated completion phase practice.

pg. III   *... the womb of experience ...*

The Tibetan *chos 'byung* means "the place from which experience arises."

pg. 113   *That being disappears.*

Through the cultivation of compassion, doing taking and sending, and praying to your teacher, you have raised the level of energy in your attention. In that attention, emotional reactions are not able to hold together. As you bring attention to each being (an emotional reaction), that being disappears, like mist in the morning sun.

pg. 114   *... inner heat, magical apparition, dream, and sheer clarity ...*

The name Kagyu is an abbreviation for the phrase "the lineage of the four instructions," the four instructions being inner heat, magical apparition, dream, and sheer clarity. These four practices are the core of all the Kagyu traditions. In the Six Practices of Naropa or The Six Practices of Niguma, two other practices are added, transference and bardo.

pg. 118   *... Mahayana Mind Training and taking and sending ...*

For Mahayana Mind Training, *Reflections on Silver River* provides a concise but comprehensive account of the essential points in the form of a translation and commentary of Tokmé Zongpo's *37 Practices of a Bodhisattva*. For taking and sending, *The Great Path of Awakening* is Jamgön Kongtrul's meditation manual for this practice. For more detailed instruction, see Chapter 8 in *Wake Up to Your Life*.

pg. 123   *Release of internal material*

For one description of the process that takes place when internal material releases, see *Wake Up to Your Life*, pg. 200–202.

CHAPTER 7

pg. 127   *Deities of the Five Tantras*

Deities of the Five Tantras is a practice that developed late in the Vajrayana tradition of India. It brings together the deities of five separate tantras into one practice. The five tantras are Lord of Secrets (Guhyasamaja), Mystical Enchantment (Mahamaya), Great Vajra (Hevajra), Wheel of Bliss (Chakrasamvara), and Vajra Terrifier (Vajrabhairava).

pg. 127   *Just do the ritual.*

Relatively little is written about protector practice other than instructions for ritual practice. Like meditation deities, most of them come from old Indian religions. More than a few do double duty, acting as both personal deities and protectors.

pg. 128   *... honor the gods through ritual ...*

Cf. Shinto. The indigenous religion of Japan, Shinto is based almost entirely on the correct performance of rituals, whether they be the short rituals a visitor does as part of his or her visit to a shrine or the elaborate dances and offering rituals performed by Shinto priests.

pg. 129   *... a tripartite structure: opening, body, and closing ...*

The opening practice is refuge and awakening mind, refuge to set your direction and awakening mind to set your motivation.

The body of practice is no reference, that is, whatever practice you are doing, you drop into non-conceptual knowing and practice from there.

The closing practice is dedication, dedicating the goodness and understanding from the ritual to the welfare of all beings. The closing section usually includes three different kinds of prayers: dedication prayers, aspiration prayers, and good fortune prayers.

pg. 129   *It is used in every tradition of Tibetan Buddhism.*

This prayer even found its way into *Star Wars*. In *The Return of the Jedi*, the ewoks speak in digitally distorted Tibetan. If you listen carefully, you can catch a few phrases here and there, including the opening words of this prayer.

pg. 129   *... inner offerings and tormas ...*

Both inner offerings and tormas nourish the gods with timeless awareness.

pg. 130   *... the five meats and the five elixirs ...*

The five meats are beef, dog, elephant, horse, and human flesh. The five elixirs are feces, urine, blood, semen, and marrow. According to Kalu Rinpoche, the five meats are of the nature of the five male buddhas and the five elixirs are of the nature of the five female buddhas. They melt together, are consecrated with the timeless awareness of all buddhas, and become a sea of liquid timeless awareness that transforms ordinary experience based in ignorance into empty experience based in timeless awareness.

pg. 130   *... five aspects of awakening, and the five aspects of timeless awareness ...*

The five aspects of awakening are the five primordial buddhas (Akshobya, Ratnasambhava, Amitabha, Amogasiddhi, and Vairocana), who arise as the transformations of the five heaps (Sanskrit skandhas). The five aspects of time-less awareness are mirror-like, balancing, distinguishing, effective, and all-encompassing timeless awareness. They arise as the transformation of the five emotional reactions, anger, instinct (stupidity), desire, jealousy, and pride.

pg. 136   *… seven-born saints …*

A rishi or seer who has been a rishi in seven consecutive lives. Such a person was deemed to be of such profound virtue that his or her bones were so saturated with goodness that they were indestructible. The original vajra was made from the bones of one such rishi.

pg. 138   *Let the mantra chain carry your devotion right into Mahakala's heart.*

The power of any communication resides in its emotional energy. In this prac-tice you draw on the emotional energy of devotion to power your communica-tion with Mahakala.

pg. 138   *… his wrath, compassion, and power …*

Vajrayana is based in the bodhisattva ethic. How often has the unthinking stu-pidity of others, injustices in the social order, or the perversity of people who harm themselves while they harm others left you seething with rage? That anger is the wrath of the protectors. It arises from compassion. The protectors see clearly. They cut through reactivity and confusion and know what is going on. Then they do what needs to be done.

pg. 149   *Burnt-offering rituals primarily address troublemakers.*

The original Indian tantras included many ancillary rituals for making peace with troublemakers. In the three-year retreat, several such rituals are part of the daily schedule.

pg. 149   *… a category of gods and demons who create problems …*

Many people think that Buddhism is a religion without gods. It is not. His-torically, when Buddhism came into a culture, it did not seek to eliminate the indigenous religions. The native gods and demons were placated, subdued, or converted, but rarely banished, exiled, or destroyed. Instead, Buddhism brought a mystical dimension to the indigenous practices, a move to the ver-tical dimension.

In Vajrayana culture the gods are many and profuse. Buddhas and bodhisattvas reside in domains of awakening (buddha realms) beyond all conception, human or otherwise. Guardians, protectors, and dakinis are active in this world, but they embody an understanding that is not of this world. They have their spe-cial places on the margins of society—charnel grounds, caves, groves, moun-tains, and rivers. Other gods are in this world and of this world. They also dwell in mountains, cliffs, lakes, or groves. Jealous and protective, they generate peace and good fortune in their domains when they are happy and trouble and problems when they are not. Still other spirits, whether demons or ghosts, bring famine, disease, earthquake, flood, or war when they are unhappy or displeased. Other spirits keep the body in balance and cause mental or physical illness when they are neglected. And then there are those who are angry, bitter, jealous, greedy, or proud. These troublemakers have no idea what they are doing or why. Usually hungry ghosts, they feel they are owed something and do not care how they collect it.

In Buddhism there is no notion of false gods. The gods in every Buddhist culture are reflections of the richness and complexity of life, in all its physical, emotional, and spiritual dimensions. Whether they are seen as expressions of awareness, awakening, or compassion, or of the deep and unfathomable forces that guide us in our spiritual practice, or of possession by anger, jealousy, or greed, or of the energy and power of mountains, winds, or seas, or of earthquakes, floods, or forest fires, or of imbalances such as plague, pestilence, emotional disturbance, or demonic possession, or of sources of good or bad luck, bad judgment or bad choices, all the gods come from the empty clarity of mind itself.

The rituals themselves are usually set up as offerings to the four guests: buddhas and bodhisattvas because they are worthy of respect, protectors and guardians because they are bound by oaths, sentient beings because they struggle in their lives, and troublemakers because they are greedy and resentful.

pg. 149   *The purpose of this ritual …*

For the troublemakers, the protectors have already shown what to do. You use the four kinds of awakening activity, or the four levels of conflict. You ask them to leave you alone and, in turn, you promise to respect them and leave them alone. If that does not work, you make offerings — burnt offerings because these spirits do not eat solid food. They can only eat smells. If nourishment fails, you threaten them, and, if that fails, you release them from their pain and struggles.

pg. 149   *… white and sweet foods …*

The three white foods are milk, yoghurt, and curds. The three sweet foods are honey, sugar, and molasses.

pg. 150   *… the four visions …*

The four stages of tögal, or direct crossing, in which the experience of mind nature unfolds in the practitioner.

pg. 150   *… the youthful vase body …*

An epithet for awakening in the Nyingma tradition.

pg. 151   ... *the major and minor marks* ...

The 32 major and 80 minor physical characteristics of an awakened person, of a buddha.

CHAPTER 8

pg. 162   ... *as soon as the mind moves* ...

This paragraph is about the immediate mind (Tib. *de ma thag pa'i yid*) or the instantaneous mind, a ninth consciousness that is sometimes added to the eight consciousnesses.

pg. 162   *Karma Chakmé*

A 17th century master from Eastern Tibet, he is probably best known for his Mountain Dharma (available in English), his prayer for rebirth in The Realm of Bliss (Sukhavati), Amitabha's domain of awakening, and his Sky Dharma cycle of teaching on The Realm of Bliss.

pg. 163   *You practice mindfulness* ...

There are many ways of practicing mindfulness. This sentence refers to the practice of noting what you are experiencing in each moment.

pg. 168   *The 37 Practices of a Bodhisattva*

See *Reflections on Silver River* or https://unfetteredmind.org/37-practices-of-a -bodhisattva/

pg. 168   *30 Pieces of Sincere Advice*

See https://unfetteredmind.org/longchenpas-30-pieces-of-sincere-advice/

pg. 169   *The fourth and final level is called "no practice."*

The four stages are single mind, simplicity, one taste, and no practice.

pg. 170   *Mindfulness is knowing what you are doing. Awareness is being aware of what is going on.*

These are formal definitions of mindfulness and awareness in the Tibetan tradition. In this context, awareness refers to alertness or attentiveness (Tib. *shes bzhin*), not direct awareness (*rig pa*) or timeless awareness (*ye shes*).

pg. 173   *Devotion Pierces My Heart*

See https://unfetteredmind.org/devotion-pierces-my-heart/

pg. 174   *... mind nature shows you what to do.*

In my second three-year retreat, Kalu Rinpoche directed me to study "Recognizing Your Mind as the Guru," a song by one of the Shangpa patriarchs.

See https://unfetteredmind.org/recognizing-mind-as-the-guru/

pg. 174   *Rest in the experience of things without seeing them as things.*

All the matter of the world, living and not living,
Arise as objects to my eyes.
Let me rest in the appearance of things, without seeing them as things.
Empty clarity without fixation is the deity's form.
I pray to my teacher, empty appearance, natural and free.

All the sounds of the world, pleasant or unpleasant,
Echo as objects in my ears.
Let me rest in the silence in sound, inconceivable and inexpressible.
Silence in sound, without beginning or end, is the speech of the awakened.
I pray to my teacher, empty sound, natural and free.

All the thoughts from emotional reactions, the five poisons,
Move as objects in my mind.
Let me rest without craft, not awaiting them, not chasing them.
When I let movement settle naturally, it releases in true presence.
I pray to my teacher, empty awareness, natural and free.
— Padmasambhava, *Prayer in Seven Chapters*

pg. 176   *Return to what is already there and rest.*

To live practice with this instruction, it helps to have fully assimilated at least one practice framework. The framework may be the six realms, the five elements, the four immeasurables, your meditation deity, magical apparition, or any other.

pg. 177   *Pawo Tsulak Trengwa*

dpa' bo gtsug lag phreng ba, (1504–1566), the second Pawo incarnation, was a historian in the Karma Kagyu tradition, a disciple of Mikyö Dorje, the 8th Karmapa, and a teacher to Wangchuk Dorje, the 9th Karmapa.

pg. 178   *The eight concerns*

The eight conventional concerns are happiness and unhappiness, gain and loss, fame and obscurity, and respect and disdain.

GLOSSARY

Vajrayana evolved in an age and a culture very different from our own. Many teachers, translators, and practitioners are actively exploring the best way, or even a good way, to express the ideas and practices of this tradition in our culture. This book is, in part, my contribution to that exploration.

The purpose of this glossary is to help you, the reader, connect the choices I have made with vocabulary you may have already encountered in other books. It works in two ways.

First, if you know Tibetan, this glossary gives you the actual Tibetan (in italics, following Wylie's Romanization) for Vajrayana terms such as connection-being or mediated completion phase. Second, if you don't know Tibetan, the glossary gives you common alternative translations.

ATTENTION

ting nge 'dzin (Skt. samadhi), also translated as absorption. It means undistracted attention. The word is used in many contexts—as the union of mindfulness (*dran pa*) and awareness (*shes bzhin*), as the union of calm abiding (*zhi gnas*) and insight (*lhag mthong*), or as the joining of the mind with an object such as water to experience water samadhi.

ATTENTION-BEING

ting nge 'dzin sems dpa' (Skt. samadhisattva), the third of the three beings, the three aspects of a deity in creation phase practice. The attention-being usually takes the form of the seed syllable or sigil of the deity. See connection-being and awareness-being.

AWAKENING MIND

byang chub sems (Skt. bodhicitta), the union of compassion and emptiness and the basis of Mahayana practice.

AWARENESS-BEING

ye shes sems dpa' (Skt. jñanasattva), the second of the three beings, the three aspects of a deity in creation phase practice. Literally, the timeless awareness-being, the primordial deity that unites with the connection-being.

BARDO

bar do, an intermediate period. It usually refers to the period between death and birth, but it can also mean the period between any two other states.

COMPLETION PHASE

rdzogs rim, the second of the two phases of deity practice. In this phase, the experience of being the deity is completed with the experience of being empty.

CONNECTION-BEING

dam tshig sems dpa' (Skt. samayasattva), the first of the three beings, the three aspects of a deity in creation phase practice. It is also translated as commitment-being. The connection-being is the form of the deity that arises in the clear empty knowing in your own mind and is the way you connect with being the deity.

CREATION PHASE

bskyed rim, the first of the two phases of deity practice. In this phase, the practitioner becomes the deity.

DEITY

yi dam, meditation deity, the god or deity that arises through the intention of awakening in a form that helps beings free themselves from the vicissitudes of samsara.

DEMONIC OBSESSIONS (FOUR)

bdud bzhi, the four maras. They are obsession with death (Skt. Yama), obsession with reactive emotions (Skt. kleśa), obsession with psychophysical existence (Skt. skandha), and obsession with peak experience or divine child (Skt. deva-putra). The Tibetan word *bdud* (pron. dü) is defined as a being who harms sentient beings and stands in opposition to the spiritual. Psychologically speaking, this kind of demon is a personification of forces that impede spiritual growth.

DEVOTION

mos gus (pron. mö gü) Literally, respectful appreciation, this emotion plays an important role in Vajrayana practice, particularly in teacher-union and related practices.

DIRECT AWARENESS

rig pa (Skt. vidya), also translated as awareness, a natural knowing undistorted by emotional reactivity and conceptual confusion.

DIRECT KNOWING

rtogs pa, also translated as realization. It refers to a knowing unmediated by the conceptual mind, a knowing in which knowing and known are not separated.

DIVINE PRIDE

lha'i nga rgyal, one of three qualities cultivated in creation phase practice. This term refers to the clear experience of being the deity. See glossary entries for pure clarity and pure recollection.

DZOGCHEN

rdzogs chen (a contraction of *rdzogs pa chen po*), a system of direct awareness practice based in the Nyingma traditions and adopted to a greater or lesser extent by other traditions.

EMPOWERMENT

dbang (pron. wāng), also translated as initiation. At one level, it is a ritual through which a student is brought to the point that he or she is able to engage in deity practice. At another level, it is a radical shift that moves the practitioner into mystical experience.

EMPTY EXPERIENCE

dag snang, also translated as pure experience, pure vision, or sacred outlook. The term has five distinct meanings in Tibetan.

1. A shift into experiencing life and the world as the play of timeless awareness. For this meaning dag snang is translated as empty experience. In this context, empty and pure are virtually synonymous and empty does not carry the problematic connotations that pure does in English.

2. A shift into experiencing life and the world as the deity and the deity's world. Likewise, for this shift, dag snang is translated as empty experience.

3. A visionary experience, or a visionary dream of buddhas, teachers, deities, or protectors. The word vision or the phrase visionary experience conveys the meaning here.

4. Seeing the sacred in someone or something. In this context, the word reverence is an appropriate rendering.

5. Seeing the best in someone or something. In this context, the word respect is one way to convey the meaning.

ENERGY

The word energy has been used to translate over ten different words in Tibetan. In the context of teacher-union, the Tibetan word is *byin rlabs* (pron. jin lap), which means a wave of inspirational energy. It has also been translated as blessing and might well be translated as grace. In the context of completion phrase practice, the Tibetan word is *rlung* (pron. lūng), which is analogous to *qi* in Chinese and *vayu* in Sanskrit (prana is one form of vayu). It is also sometimes translated as *wind* (its literal meaning). In the context of buddhas and protectors, the appropriate Tibetan word is sometimes *nus pa* or *nus shugs* (pron. nüpa and nüshuk), meaning capability or capability and power.

ENERGY SURGE

nyams, also translated as experience. The word has many meanings, but in the context of meditation practice, it refers to transitory experiences that arise in meditation, usually brought about by the release of energy as patterned conditioning breaks down.

ENGAGING OBLIGATION

thugs dam bskang, also translated as appeasing or pacifying, a ritual element in protector rituals in which the practitioner makes offerings to obligate the protector to perform his or her duties.

EXPERIENCE

chos (Skt. dharma) has a wide range of meanings. As a philosophical term referring to what is experienced (in contrast to its use as a term for religion), it is often translated as phenomenon.

EXPERIENTIAL KNOWING

nyams, also translated as vision or visionary experience. The term also refers to experiences of bliss, clarity, or non-thought that arise in connection with meditation practice. They are transitory and are often mistaken for direct knowing.

FAITH

dad pa, a feeling of understanding, longing, and clarity toward a spiritual figure, text, or principle. It is also translated as confidence or trust and sometimes, erroneously, as belief.

FOUR IMMEASURABLES

tshad med bzhi, also translated as the four boundless thoughts or four limitless virtues, they are loving kindness, compassion, joy, and equanimity.

FOUR LEVELS OF TANTRA

rgyud sde bzhi, four classes of tantra: ritual tantra (*bya rgyud* or kriya tantra), behavior tantra (*spyod rgyud* or charya tantra), union tantra (*rnal 'byor rgyud* or yoga tantra), and supreme union tantra (*bla med rnal 'byor rgyud* or anuttara yoga tantra)

GROUNDWORK

sngon 'gro, a set of practices that prepare a spiritual practitioner for a specific kind of meditation. This term is also translated as preliminary practices or foundational practices.

IMMEDIATE MIND

de ma thag pa'i yid, a movement that arises in the moment of perception that gives rise to the experience of subject or object, also translated as instantaneous mind.

INTERMEDIATE PERIOD

bar do, see entry for bardo.

LIVING PRACTICE

rtul zhugs and *lam du khyer ba* (lam khyer). Both terms refer to ethics, that is, the way you choose to live to develop and express your spiritual understanding.

MAGIC

sgyu ma, also translated as sorcery, enchantment, magic, illusion, or phantom.

MAGICAL APPARITION

sgyu lus, literally illusion body or magic body, often translated as illusory body, one of The Six Practices (of Naropa, Niguma, or Sukhasiddhi).

MAHAMUDRA

phyag rgya chen po, literally The Great Seal, a name for a spiritual tradition and a form of direct awareness meditation taught by Tilopa and other Indian masters and brought to Tibet in the New Translation wave (11th and 12th centuries).

MEDIATED COMPLETION PHASE

mtshan bcas rdzogs rim, also translated as completion phase with signs. It refers to entry into clear empty knowing mediated by energy transformation practices.

MIND ITSELF

sems nyid, a contraction of *sems kyi chos nyid*, the pure being of mind (Skt. citta-dharmata). It refers to a knowing unmediated by concept and in which subject and object have not separated.

MIND NATURE

sems kyi rang bzhin, nature of mind or mind nature, virtually synonymous with mind itself.

MYSTICAL

gsang and *chen po*. The former means secret or hidden and refers to practices and understandings that were hidden to non-practitioners. The latter means great and when appended to a word often signifies that the word has taken on mystical significance. Great Compassion, for instance, is an epithet for Avalokiteshvara (Chenrezi) and means that he embodies a mystical compassion, not a conventional compassion. The Great Seal (mahamudra) means a mystical seal, the seal of emptiness. Mahakala, The Great Black One, means that this protector is not an ordinary god, but is associated with mystical practice.

ORAL AUTHORIZATION

rlung, (pron. lüng), the word for energy. In this context it refers to a formal reading of the text to a student.

PATH OF METHOD

thabs lam, also translated as path of means or methodical path.

PATH OF RELEASE

grol lam, also translated as path of liberation, path of freedom, and free path.

PRACTICE TEXT

sgrub thabs (Skt. sadhana), method of practice. It usually takes the form of a text that describes the method of meditation under consideration. It is used primarily in the context of deity practice.

POWER

dngos grub (Skt. siddhi), also translated as accomplishment or success. See Chapter 3 notes.

PROTECTOR

chos skyong (Skt. dharmapala) variously translated as protector, guardian, guardian deity, defender of the teaching.

PURE CLARITY

rnam dag gsal ba, one of three qualities to be cultivated in creation phase practice. This term refers to clearly experiencing the deity's form in all its detail as your own. See pure recollection and divine pride.

PURE RECOLLECTION

rnam dag dran pa, one of three qualities to be cultivated in creation phase practice. This term refers to the clear awareness of the symbolic significance of each aspect of the deity's form. See pure clarity and divine pride.

PURIFICATION

sbyong ba, to train, study, refine, purify, and empty (of impurities). In the context of deity practice, it means to empty experience of the investment of self.

RADIATION-ABSORPTION

spro bsdu, the practice of radiating light or energy and then absorbing it. It is also translated as sending out and drawing in, projection and absorption, emanating and gathering, etc.

REACTIVITY AND CONFUSION

nyon rmongs pa'i sgrib pa dang shes bya'i sgrib pa, also translated as the two obscurations, the two veils, the veil of emotional reactions and the veil of conceptual knowing.

SIGIL

sa bon, the word for seed in Tibetan. In magical parlance, it is a sigil, that is, a "seed syllable" that embodies the intention of the magic ritual.

SIX KINDS OF BEINGS

'kor ba rigs drug, also translated as the six realms; rigs has several meanings including realm, kind, and family.

SPELL

sngags (Skt. mantra), a magical formula that is sung, chanted, or recited to invoke a deity.

SPIRITUAL

chos (Skt. dharma) has a wide range of meanings, including religion. Used as an adjective, it can mean religious or spiritual.

TEACHER-UNION PRACTICE

lama'i rnal 'byor (Skt. guru yoga), a genre of practices in which the student seeks to join his or her mind with the teacher's mind.

TIMELESS AWARENESS

ye shes (Skt. jñana), awareness that is unmediated by the conceptual mind. It is also described as panoramic, primordial, pristine, pure, or absolute and named awareness, wisdom, knowing, or wakefulness.

THE THREE SOURCES

rtswa ba gsum, also translated as The Three Roots. Guru is the source of energy, Deity the source of power, and Protector the source of action.

TORMA

gtor ma (Skt. baling), physically, an offering made from dough that is shaped, colored, and decorated according to the recipient and the purpose of the offering. Mystically, it is an offering of timeless awareness to deities and protectors.

UNMEDIATED COMPLETION PHASE

mtshan med rdzogs rim, also translated as completion phase without signs. It refers to entry into empty clear awareness unmediated by energy transformation practices.

WOMB OF EXPERIENCE

chos 'byung (pron. chö jung), also translated as womb or matrix of phenomena.

BIBLIOGRAPHY

PREVIOUSLY PUBLISHED ARTICLES

"A Way of Freedom," *Tricycle*, November, 2010
"When Energy Runs Wild," *BuddhaDharma*, November, 2011
"Prayer Without Blind Faith," *Tricycle*, December, 2015
"When the Thinking Stops," *Tricycle*, February, 2016
"How Samaya Works," *Tricycle*, November 2018

OTHER SOURCES

A Guide for the Perplexed, E.F. Schumacher, New York, Perennial Library, 1977
After Life, https://www.imdb.com/title/tt0165078/
Chuang Tzu: The Inner Chapters, trans. David Hinton, Washington, D.C., Counterpoint, 1998
Clarifying the Natural State, Dakpo Tashi Namgyal, trans. Erik Pema Kunsang, Hong Kong, Rangjung Yeshe Publications, 2001
Creation and Completion, Jamgön Kongtrul, trans. Sarah Harding, Boston, Wisdom Publications, 2002
Empowerment and the Path of Liberation, Tsele Natsog Rangdrol, trans. Erik Pema Kunsang, Nepal, Rangjung Yeshe Publications, 1993
The Great Path of Awakening, Jamgön Kongtrul, trans. Ken McLeod, Boston, Shambhala, 1987
The Long Fall, Walter Mosley, New York, Penguin Random House, 2009
Niguma: Lady of Illusion, Sarah Harding, Ithaca, USA, Snow Lion, 2011
Overcoming Barriers to Student Understanding: Threshold Concepts and Troublesome Knowledge, Jan Meyer and Ray Land, Routledge, 2006
Wake Up to Your Life, Ken McLeod, San Francisco, HarperSanFrancisco, 2001
The Way of the Bodhisattva, Shantideva, trans. Padmakara Translation Group, Boulder, Shambhala, Revised edition, 2006

Born in England in 1948, Ken McLeod grew up in Ontario, Canada. After graduating with a degree in mathematics in 1969, Ken cycled across Europe to Istanbul and then continued his journey overland to India.

In 1970 he met his principal teacher Kalu Rinpoche at his monastery near Darjeeling. There Ken began a study and practice in Tibetan Buddhism that lasted more than twenty years. He completed the traditional three-year retreat program two times, translated for many teachers, and helped set up Buddhist centers in Canada and the United States. Designated by Kalu Rinpoche in 1985 as the resident teacher of his Los Angeles center, Ken is one of the first generation of Western teachers in the Tibetan tradition and one of the few to be authorized to transmit the full scope of these teachings.

After his teacher's passing, Ken moved away from the hierarchical structures of Asian Buddhism and explored new approaches. In 1990, he founded Unfettered Mind in Los Angeles. His approach of one-on-one consultations roiled the Buddhist world in the early '90s, but was quickly recognized as a viable way to teach and guide students in the West. In numerous small groups in Southern California, he developed the materials that became the encyclopedic meditation manual *Wake Up to Your Life*. In addition to retreats and courses, he conducted a number of teacher development programs. He continues to mentor teachers on an informal basis.

From 1999 to 2017, Ken headed a consulting practice that focused on leadership skills, team building, and personal and organizational effectiveness. He has worked with senior executives in Fortune 100 companies and a wide range of organizations including HBO, Volvo, and ReadyPac.

Now retired from formal teaching, he lives in Northern California where he hikes and writes. His writings and translations include *The Great Path of Awakening* (1987), *Wake Up to Your Life* (2001), *An*

Arrow to the Heart (2007), *Reflections on Silver River* (2014), *A Trackless Path* (2017), and *The Magic of Varjayana* (2022), as well as a corpus of articles and translations in *Tricycle* and other Buddhist magazines. An archive of Ken's work including podcasts from retreats and classes can be found at unfetteredmind.org.

www.ingramcontent.com/pod-product-compliance
Lightning Source LLC
Chambersburg PA
CBHW020441130626

46549CB00001B/245